To Know Each Other and Be Known: Women's Writing Workshops

by Beverly Tanenhaus,
with poems by workshop participants

Out & Out Books
476 Second Street
Brooklyn, New York 11215

Copyright © 1978 Beverly Tanenhaus
All rights for contributors' poems return to the authors.

Phantasia for Elvira Shatayev copyright © 1975 Adrienne Rich
Amazon Poetry: An Anthology. (Out & Out Books)
(reprinted by permission of the author).

Power copyright © 1975 Audre Lorde
Between Our Selves. (Eidolon Editions)
(reprinted by permission of the author).

Note: Adrienne Rich's prose poem, *Women and Honor: Some Notes On Lying,* referred to in the text, has been published as a pamphlet by Motheroot Press, Pittsburgh (1977).

No part of this work may be reproduced or utilized in any form or by any means, electronic or mechanical, including photocopying, recording, or by any information storage and retrieval system, without permission in writing from the publisher.

Production: Susan Dansker
Cover Design: Lynne Reynolds
Typesetting: Ellen Shapiro

Photo Credits:
James D. Parsons, Jr.,: Pages x, 34, 69
Barbara Adams: Pages viii, Back Cover
Holly Russell: Page 57

ISBN: 0-918-31405-4
Address all orders and inquiries to:
Out & Out Books
476 Second Street
Brooklyn, New York 11215

Produced at The Print Center, Inc., Box 1050, Brooklyn, N.Y. 11202, a non-profit printing facility for literary and arts-related publications. Funded by The New York State Council on the Arts and the National Endowment for the Arts.

To my mother and father–
  I've moved away from your circles
    to speak out
  And you've moved into my circles
    to hear me

Contents

Letter by Martha Ficklen	vi
Author's Note	vii
Womanroots	ix
Beginnings	1
The First Time	2
Adrienne Rich	
Phantasia For Elvira Shatayev	4
In The Classroom	6
Taking Ourselves Seriously	13
Liberating Ourselves From Our Secrets	16
Results Immediate and Drastic	18
Barbara Bickel	
I was promised	19
Dale Darling	
Evolution: Then and Now	20
Breakthrough Poems	20
Holly Russell	
trapped	20
Nana	21
After Statement	22
Dianne Chiddister	
Together	23
Revision of *Together*	23
Interview	23
Mary Ann Scheuhing	
An Imagination on the Genetics of Suicide	26
Recollections of My Mother	26
Aldona Middlesworth	
He sits in a kaleidoscope	27
Instructions on how to sell roses in the fine restaurants, to the gentlemen for their ladies	29
Towards the New Feminist Ethic	30
Audre Lorde	
Power	31
After Statement	32
Melanie Perish	
Turning Away	35
Beverly Tanenhaus	
The Indulgence of Love	36
Linda Brown	
Gathering A Self	39
Conflict	42

Friendship   **48**
  Beverly Tanenhaus
    The Last Love Song   52
  Paula Gills
    Singing For My Sisters   56
Re-Entry   **58**
  Elizabeth Kaye
    After Hearing Kate Millet   62
  Melanie Perish
    Arriving for a Visit   63
    To Look at My Hands and See   64
    After Statement   65
  Martha Ficklen
    Aunt   66
  Beverly Tanenhaus
    To The Daughter I Became
      Who Gave Birth To The Mother I Needed   67

Among my reasons for coming to this Workshop were wanting to focus for myself what I want to do with writing and wanting to find out how committed to writing I'm willing to be.

The experience here has been overwhelming. My first reaction to the people here was, "These women are saying things I want to hear!" The open, receptive atmosphere has held up. The conversations have been good. Articulation and sharing of ourselves with each other has continued from classtime into free time, at meals, walking (climbing) from place to place, in the dorm lounge at night. Even in the toilet the dialog goes on. Not always with the same intensity, but at a level of candor and trust that is really important.

There's been time for talking and time for writing. I've made pages and pages of notes, things I want to write, ways I want to try to do it, ideas I want to work with. I know myself a little better. I accept myself with a little less protest. In these two weeks I've felt very much reinforced as a person and as a writer and as a woman.

I can appreciate the careful attention to details, the planning that went into getting this together, but most of all, I can appreciate the energy and enthusiasm spent in making us welcome. Classes allow for positive, helpful criticism, without competition. Our work has been taken seriously.

Beverly has told us she wanted us here because she was lonely. I'm here because I was lonely, too. Loneliness is something we all can share and understand and use to create that sense of community of women who are willing to know each other and be known.

Martha Ficklen
Women's Writing Workshop '75

Author's Note

I have tried to speak in a collective voice, drawing on the response of participants over the past two years in order to document an experience genuinely communal and continuing. At the same time, I've hoped that participants' remarks have extended the limitations of my own point of view.

Almost without exception, I've restricted my quotes to women directly involved in the Workshops. Comments from guest speakers were recorded on the scene in informal class discussions. I interviewed Audre Lorde in April '77 since I did not record what turned out to be her extraordinary class visit at the '76 Pine Lake Workshop. The poems or parts of poems I've quoted by Adrienne Rich and Audre Lorde were ones they actually included in their Workshop readings.

In this book, as in the Workshops themselves, my perspective fluctuates. Although I have identified primarily as a teacher/administrator, I have also responded as a writer, like the other women I met, struggling to retrieve and clarify my experiences through the language. For this reason, along with participants' work, I've included several of my own poems which could not have been written, nor fully understood, without the women of the Workshops.

I would like to thank participants for sharing their reflections with me and for allowing their insights to become a matter of public record. I would also like to thank those women who generously read and commented on the text. Special appreciation goes to Jim Lawrence, formerly a dean at Hartwick College, whose enthusiasm helped launch the first Workshop, to Nancy Lord, secretary, and to Evalyn Bates, currently Dean of Special Programs at Hartwick, whose personal and administrative support has allowed the program to continue and expand.

Finally, my deepest thanks to Joan Larkin, editor of Out & Out Books, whose faith in me not only gave me the publishing resources but also the self-confidence to offer this book as a primer and joyous precedent for the proliferation of women's writing communities.

Beverly Tanenhaus
June, 1977

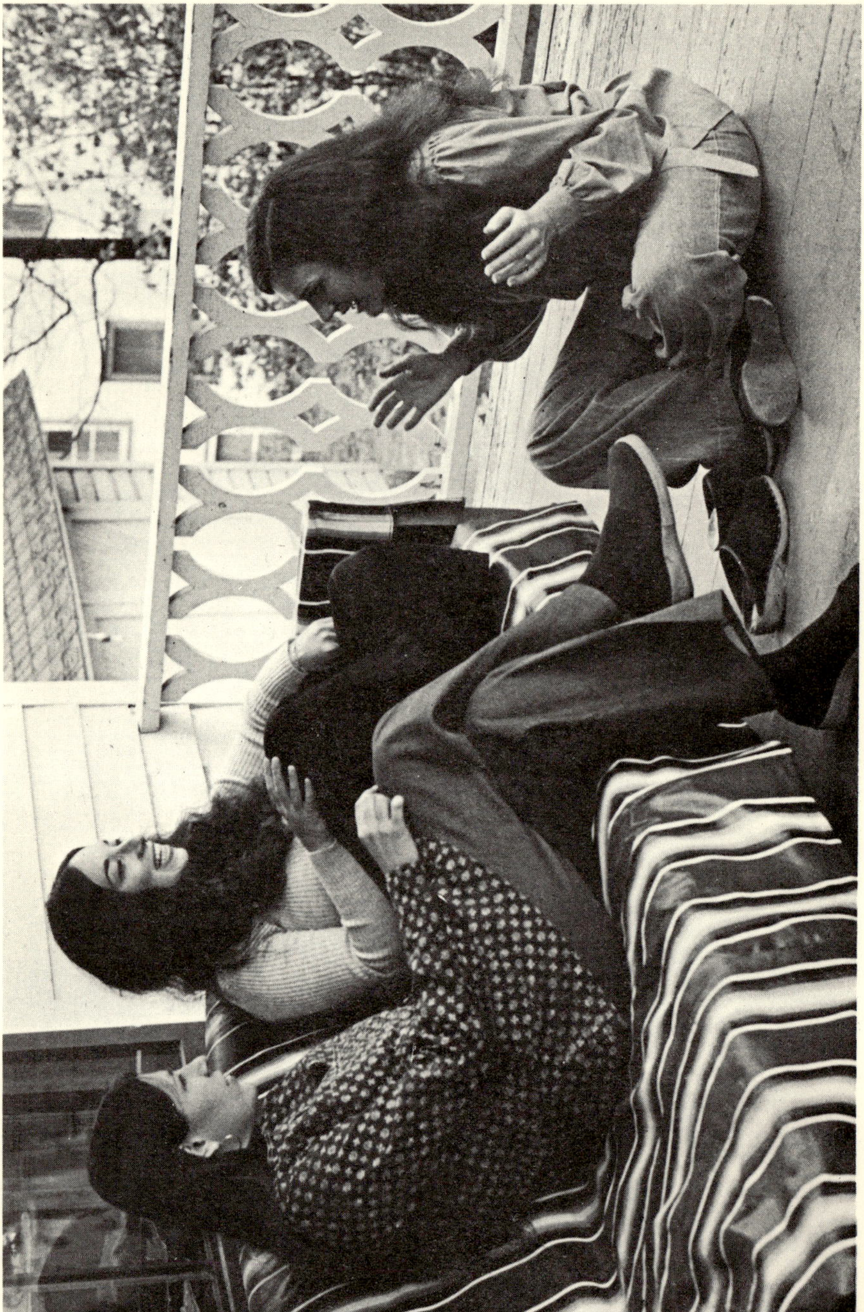

WOMANROOTS

1975

Instructor	Workshop	Guest Speakers	Place
Beverly Tanenhaus	Combined Poetry & Fiction	Adrienne Rich Toni Morrison	Hartwick Main Campus

1976, First Session

Beverly Tanenhaus	Poetry	Adrienne Rich Alice Walker	Hartwick Main Campus
Joanna Russ	Fiction	Elaine Gill, Crossing Press	

1976, Second Session

Beverly Tanehaus	Combined Poetry & Fiction	Audre Lorde Grace Paley Anne Pride, KNOW Press	Pine Lake Campus

1977, First Session

Beverly Tanehaus	Combined Poetry & Fiction	Robin Morgan Alice Walker Anne Pride, KNOW Press	Hartwick Main Campus
Mary Jane Moffat	Journal Writing		

1977, Second Session

Beverly Tanenhaus	Combined Poetry & Fiction	Audre Lorde Grace Paley June Arnold, Daughters, Inc.	Pine Lake Campus

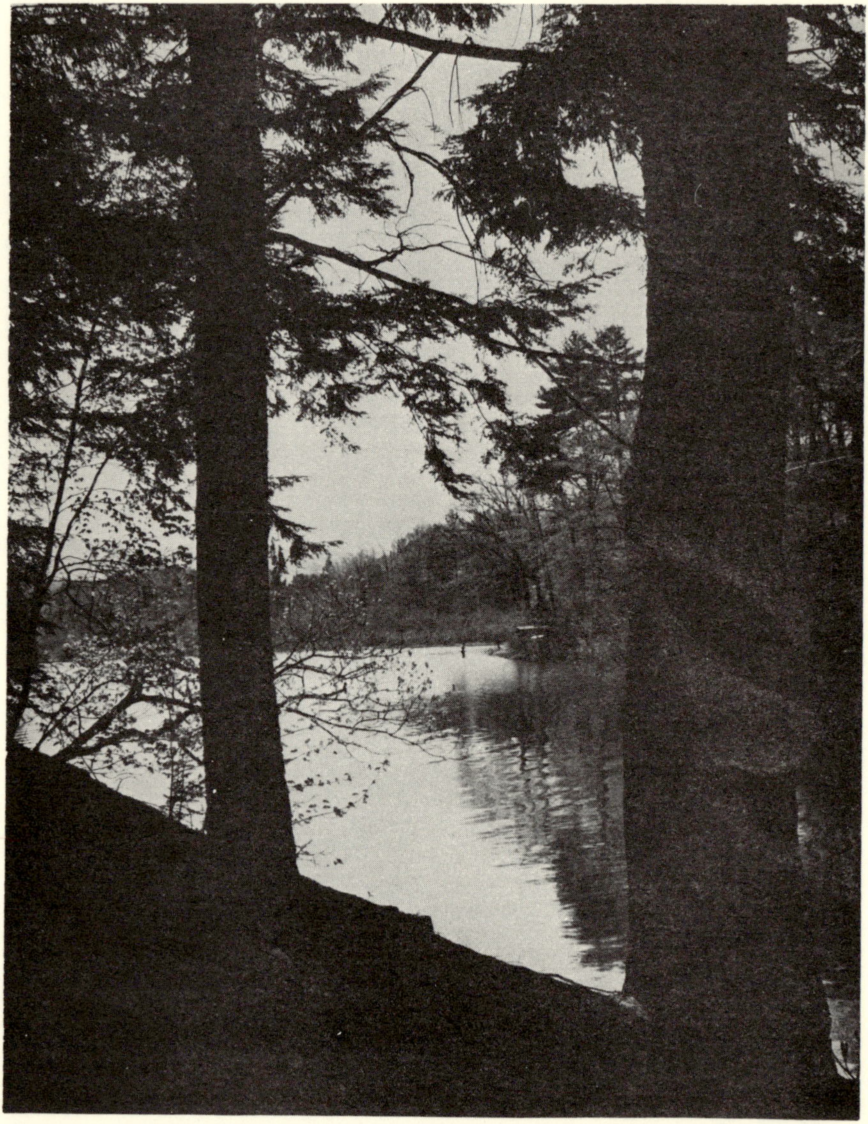

Beginnings

On June 22, 1975, a group of strangers gathered outside a modern geometrical structure known on campus as "the building with breasts." In this fitting locale, women from all over the country came to live and work in community for the first national two-week Women's Writing Workshop. I peered at name tags, connecting new faces with the manuscripts I had studied for several weeks, incredulous that all the women I had expected for a year had shown up.

The idea for a Women's Writing Workshop began as an antidote to my own isolation in the small town I had dubbed Sleepy Hollow, where my insistence on being called "Ms." created a local controversy in 1973. Later, the Workshop became a kind of joy ride, approved by a maverick male dean (later fired), and planned with the abandon reserved for my most outrageous fantasies. Twenty-four hours before the national contingent arrived, I finally admitted that the Workshop was actually going to take place. Before, that would have been too dangerous; crowded with "feminine" anxieties, I might have stopped planning such a momentous event.

At this point, I was negotiating travel arrangements by phone with guest poet Adrienne Rich, whose friendly voice was only partially distinct from the awesome poems I had studied for years. From Adrienne, I requested—with the presumption of the desperate—that she act as my sounding board, letting me verbalize my misgivings, expectations, hopes for this new project. She agreed with enthusiasm, and my first analysis of the phenomenon of women's writing communities began.

Now, only two years later, I am amazed at the self-confident words I have just written to prospective participants for the third annual Women's Writing Workshops, scheduled in two sessions at Hartwick College for summer 1977 with courses in Journal Writing as well as Creative Writing.

I welcome your interest in the Women's Writing Workshops and would like to tell you more about this experience. As a woman-defined program where we live and work together for two weeks, the Workshops try to provide what philosopher Mary Daly calls a boundary space of women's community. Temporarily away from the culture at large, as readers and writers we have the opportunity to concentrate on our own interests as first priority, to listen and speak to one another without interruption. Crucially, the Workshops provide a meeting ground for interesting women and generate lasting friendships that, for many of us, act as sustenance when we leave. [From my open letter to '77 participants]

The three Workshops that have since taken place have transformed the surprises of WWW '75 into the calm projections for summer '77. The leisurely insights of retrospective analysis, and the more painful dramatic wisdom sometimes forced by confrontation, have tempered what was for us in 1975 the unanticipated daily euphoria that is still changing our lives. I realize that I am documenting a process that is rapidly, almost imperceptibly, being absorbed into a feminist sophistication generating its own complexities and expectations. I feel that I must write this book now, or we won't remember how we began.

The First Time

> Now we are ready
> and each of us knows it   I have never loved
> like this   I have never seen
> my own forces so taken up and shared
> and given back
>
> Adrienne Rich, Phantasia for Elvira Shatayev

On the third day of WWW '75 we listened to Adrienne Rich describe a specific historical event in the voice of Elvira Shatayev, the "leader of a women's climbing team all of whom died in a storm on Lenin Peak, August 1974." As these lines about other women drifted to us, we heard words read aloud for the first time that almost syllable by syllable moved us to the core; we claimed this poem as our own. The following week, in this same brown-carpeted, spanking new auditorium, we would be told by guest novelist Toni Morrison that "Women don't know what they know, don't use what they know, don't respect what they know."

But that evening, as I looked into the audience—my Workshop, a group of 25 women clustered together on the floor in front of the stage, a thick scattering of Hartwick faculty and Oneonta residents sitting far behind them—I felt a re-connection with my power as a competent, caring woman that almost tangibly surfaced each day as exhilaration and strength. I had found my community, been confirmed in my individual value, and collectively was hard at work with other women to record as accurately and eloquently as possible the untold stories of our lives.

> What we were to learn   was simply   what we had
> up here   as out of all words   that yes   gathered
> its forces   fused itself   and only just in time
>
> Adrienne Rich, Phantasia for Elvira Shatayev

I did not immediately understand how subversive our excitement was. In the beginnings of becoming woman-defined, in our refusal to value our lives exclusively by the men who loved us, in our recognition that as women, we had been for each other a forbidden resource only now openly acknowledged as worthy of each other's attention, support, and love, we were in drastic contradiction to the patriarchy.

For the first time I realized my role as a woman in society; I developed a social consciousness here. I was amazed by my own reluctance to join into group interactions, originating from my past conditioning which suggested that men had more to say than women that was worth sharing. I realized that I have been wronged, that my life has been dictated by false concepts. I've learned to love myself as a woman and realize the potential of other women to fulfill some of my basic emotional as well as intellectual needs.

Holly Russell

During the Workshop I feared that I and others would place too much emphasis upon a two-week support system of artificial intimacy. But I find that the sense of communion I felt within the group remains as an important symbol of what is possible in other contexts as well as a memory of something that was real, though brief. Most important, perhaps, is the knowledge that I have respected interaction over a significant period of time among women. I have been truly sexist on this score in the past and needed to live it to believe it.   Clara Jones

At the guest readings the following summer, I would be obsessed with administrative detail, furious that no one had provided a water pitcher and glass for the speaker, juggling the next day's class and airplane schedules. But, that summer, we were alive with the energy of claiming our lives, perhaps for the first time, with Rich as the model, acknowledging our strength and daring to be strong.

Adrienne Rich was the first person to make me realize the need for a woman writer to demand a typewriter of her own, a desk and, if she is extremely forceful, a room of her own.   Pat McElligott

We are women steeped in a culture that trivializes, repudiates, or overlooks female accomplishments, that insists our role models are Lady Clairol, Betty Crocker, or Sleeping Beauty. Our exposure to each other at the Workshop began a rebirth of our better, truer selves that we confirmed and reflected back to each other day by day.

We know now we have always been in danger
down in our separateness
and now up here together   but till now
we had not touched our strength
                          Adrienne Rich, Phantasia for Elvira Shatayev

I keep wondering since the Workshop how many of us feel that something in our lives has irrevocably changed. I'm not even sure what has changed for me. I look at my writing much more critically now; I feel completely free to say that writing takes precedence over socializing or many other things. But what I feel best about is the realization that out of 25 women, 22 were able to enter a bond of sisterhood which transcended age, politics, sexual orientation, even talent. It might not have lasted if we'd stayed longer; it probably wouldn't have, to the same extent. But it happened, and that makes me feel that my concept of what feminism can mean is rooted in reality.   Sherry Redding

Adrienne Rich
Phantasia For Elvira Shatayev

> *(leader of a women's climbing team, all of whom died in a storm on Lenin Peak, August 1974. Later, Shatayev's husband found and buried the bodies.)*

The cold felt cold until our blood
grew colder   then the wind
died down and we slept

If in this sleep I speak
it's with a voice no longer personal
(I want to say   with voices)
When the wind tore   our breath from us at last
we had no need of words
For months   for years   each one of us
had felt her own *yes*   growing in her
slowly forming   as she stood at windows   waited
for trains   mended her rucksack   combed her hair
What we were to learn   was simply   what we had
up here   as out of all words   that *yes*   gathered
its forces   fused itself   and only just in time
to meet a *No* of no degrees
the black hole   sucking the world in

I feel you climbing toward me
your cleated bootsoles leaving   their geometric bite
colossally embossed   on microscopic crystals
as when I trailed you in the Caucasus
Now I am further
ahead   than either of us dreamed   anyone would be
I have become

the white snow packed like asphalt by the wind
the women I love   lightly flung   against the mountain
that blue sky
our frozen eyes unribboned   through the storm
we could have stitched that blueness   together   like a quilt

You come (I know this)   with your love   your loss
strapped to your body   with your tape-recorder   camera
ice-pick   against advisement
to give us burial in the snow   and in your mind
While my body lies out here
flashing like a prism   into your eyes
how could you sleep   You climbed here for yourself
we climbed for ourselves

When you have buried us   told your story
ours does not end   we stream
into the unfinished   the unbegun
the possible
Every cell's core of heat   pulsed out of us
into the thin air   of the universe
the armature of rock beneath these snows
this mountain   which has taken   the imprint of our minds
through changes elemental and minute
as those we underwent
to bring each other here
choosing ourselves   each other   and this life
whose every breath   and grasp   and further foothold
is somewhere   still eneacted   and continuing

In the diary I wrote: *Now we are ready*
and each of us knows it   I have never loved
like this   I have never seen
my own forces so taken up and shared
and given back
After the long training   the early sieges
we are moving almost effortlessly in our love

In the diary as the wind   began to tear
at the tents over us   I wrote:
We know now we have always been in danger
down in our separateness
and now up here together   but till now
we had not touched our strength

In the diary torn from my fingers I had written:
What does love mean
what does it mean   "to survive"
A cable of blue fire ropes our bodies
burning together in the snow   We will not live
to settle for less   We have dreamed of this
all of our lives

In The Classroom

Format

Despite my anonymity as a published poet, I trusted my gifts as a teacher, knowing my critical insight, my passion for taking people seriously as they struggle with the power of their own experiences and the beauty of the language. With five years of teaching creative writing behind me, I felt prepared to meet my students, these strangers pilgrimaging enormously long distances to a small town whose outstanding distinction is its proximity to the Baseball Hall of Fame. In '75, when 230 women inquired about 25 Workshop spaces, I felt reassured that my meticulous planning had attracted women who were willing to take a chance on me.

On the Main Campus, we met for classes in "the building with breasts," an air-conditioned structure only a short walk from the dormitory where most participants lived. We faced each other in a comfortable informal classroom. Occasionally, the bluest sky drifted by the picture windows. Whether sprawled in faded jeans across giant yellow beanbags or seated upright on the sofas in a dress and heels, we all honored a few specific rules. I wanted to create a friendly but professional atmosphere as quickly as possible where we mutually valued our writing and our time. Classes began promptly at 10 a.m. I regarded anyone who sauntered in late as breaking our contract and disrupting the class.

In addition to punctuality, I also requested that participants present legible, accurately typed copies of their work to me and to the class. A sloppy manuscript needlessly confuses the reader, diverting attention away from criticizing a piece merely to decipher it. If a workshop leader allows a woman to present, for example, a poem with numerous scrawled revisions toppling into the margins, she is reinforcing the writer's lack of respect for her work and for her audience.

Each day we discussed work by two participants, roughly dividing class into two one-hour sessions on each writer, with a short break in between. I was careful to give writers equal time; this meant that we might discuss two poems by A and one longer poem by B. Each woman was encouraged to xerox extra work which, though it was not scheduled for class discussion, we would all read beforehand. This allowed us to critique a particular piece thoroughly in class, and at the same time develop a bit more familiarity with the author's work in general. The extra xeroxes also inspired informal workshops among the students later in the dorm.

We were careful to refer to the speaker of a piece as "the narrator" rather than use the author's name. Not only was this more accurate critically (often a first person narrator is a personality distinct from the author) but it also provided a distance that honored the individual's privacy and encouraged objectivity among readers intimate with the writer. The writer agreed to remain silent until we had finished our critique of her work. I realize that we can manipulate critical feedback by sharing only our safest work, by altering responses through hostile body language or through an intrusive charm that deflects attention away from work to personality. Nonetheless, this method allowed us to explore multiple perspectives without being short-circuited by the author's explanations. In addition, the writer was able to gauge the accessibility and impact of the piece and occasionally learn firsthand the meaning of "intentional fallacy." Afterwards, the writer criticized the class's discussion and raised any questions that she still might have about her piece.

This rule of silence also provided a safe space for the writer to listen. Spared the anxiety of having to decide whether to correct her own errors or readers' misconceptions instantly, she patiently awaited her turn to speak. If the writer were allowed to respond during discussion, comment by comment, she might be nervously apologetic or defensive. And consequently, in order not to antagonize or upset her, one would withhold or dilute critical comments.

When the writer interrupts discussion of her work, you get a repartee instead of a body of response. Discussion becomes a reaction to the person rather than the poem. It's like trying to cut material with a blunt scissors; you get off-patterns. Audre Lorde '77

When the writer prematurely shares her interpretation of her work with the group, individual readers feel expendable. "If she understands her work so thoroughly, then what does she need me for," may become an attitude of the reader that damages the intense, shared excitement that potentially bonds each woman in the room.

Every woman determined for herself what work she would present to the class; as a teacher, I'm comfortable dealing with any piece that the writer takes seriously. With the less confident women, it was particularly important for me to remain neutral on this decision. Otherwise, my reaction might have been weighted as artistic approval or rejection. It is important that a workshop leader resist participants' assuming a subordinate role, giving her more power than she actually has in judging their work or decreeing their futures as writers. We've all been apprentices far too long.

I tremendously appreciated the serious, conscientious, and non-competitive nature of your critiques, both in our private conferences and within the class structure. In no way could I ever ascertain that, for example, one poet was published and therefore merited more awe from any one of us, or that any one work deserved any more or less critical examination than another. Nancy Osborne

The lack of competition, of trying to out-radicalize one another was amazing. Unlike my university experience, home of my intellectual fathers, no pecking order was established. Instead, I felt the worth of each woman writing. Melanie Perish

I felt from you genuine enthusiasm for each of our works, at whatever level we were, not creating a higher regard for those at more advanced stages—we were all viewed by you as having validity in our work, and this is perhaps the greatest gift you could have given. Dianne Chiddister

At the same time, I clearly identified myself as discussion leader, assuming that burden of careful listening, of keeping track of comments, of making sure that everyone had a chance to speak and that feedback was consistently constructive.

You were very fair, usually making sure that everyone who had something to say was allowed to say it. You were a definite time saver, and I appreciated the way you summed up and pulled together the comments that would flit in chaos about the room. You helped tie people's comments together and often made the general ideologies clearer to the group. And it was good that still other people often would do the same. Lisa Bernstein

Like basketball players prior to the calling of a jump ball, the class would sometimes get in a turmoil. For example, people would talk simultaneously or divert the critical attention of the group. At these instants, Beverly's job was analogous to that of a referee. She would restate the theories under consideration—like a referee holding the jump ball; then the class would react upon them.   *Ruth Young.*

A workshop leader must be attuned to people who are just beginning to sail into the discussion and make a space for their comments. At the same time, the more self-confident, verbal women must not be made to feel that they are crowding the shyer types by their eloquence and perceptiveness. In the classroom, we still battle sexist stereotypes that praise an inhibited, insecure woman as beguilingly demure, and condemn a self-assured, articulate woman as overpowering. Ideally, each woman in the room is thoughtfully, comfortably contributing her comments. Then, each of us will feel her individual importance in articulating her insight, not only for the benefit of the writer but for the creation of community among us where people respond from generosity as well as shrewd, critical judgment.

This sense of community will not wholly develop if the teacher dominates discussion by speaking out first and/or by making sweeping pejorative statements such as "This poem is magnificent!"—misplaced praise in the classroom. Not only does such a comment create a star system within the workshop, but it silences women who genuinely disagree and are afraid that their comments will be construed as opposition to the teacher or as jealousy of the poet.

I don't speak first because the students are easily overawed. Either they're going to agree or disagree, but that's going to be in reference to what I've said. On the other hand, I really very much want to speak, because I have something to say and I have a feeling about the poem. What I bring is something that the writer needs too.   *Audre Lorde, '77*

As a group leader, you had some critical sense of balance between instructing us and giving us our heads. Your instruction is the challenge that set high expectations and motivated us to take ourselves seriously enough to care about the quality of our performance—even, perhaps, to push ourselves more than we otherwise might have risked. Giving us our heads is generosity that in the final analysis each of us was responsible for setting her own limits and speaking with her own voice, not yours. How do you assess the critical balance, particularly since it probably changes from day to day?   *Clara Jones*

At times I felt that you took up too much time in class with your comments (I found your summaries of comments and direction-changing intrusions to be generally helpful, however.) You were an excellent critic, but I felt that the class time should have been primarily focused on students, and some of the instructor's comments might have been saved for conferences or written criticism.   Paula Gills

My contribution is not to tell a woman everything I know about her work but to figure out what I know about her work that she can use. This implies giving focused critical feedback without overwhelming the piece with my own impressions or dominating the discussion. Often, I find it useful to state my own opinions about the piece along with a careful presentation of contradictory points of view. Then, I ask the workshop how they feel about each perspective.

Craft

Although I closely followed class discussions and made thematic suggestions in personal conferences, I gave no specific writing assignments during the Workshop. I assumed that each person had arrived with a backlog of writing, or that she would use our two weeks as a welcome break in routine to create new work. We also freely mined each other's writing for potential topics in our own work, a process I consider inspiration.

Certain teaching methods are, to a degree, the result of personality and metabolism. I didn't give assignments because they didn't occur to me; furthermore, I remember my few required themes in graduate school as a forced march ending in an embarrassingly poor performance. I also discouraged unfocused technical discussions or minutely-rendered background anecdotes. These topics tempt many beginners as an elegant way to avoid writing and criticizing writing. Instead, I closely examined submitted work and illustrated technique through the examples at hand. Somebody's short story would stimulate discussion on the advantages and limitations of a particular narrative perspective; another person's poem would invite our comparison of traditional metaphor with feminist imagery.

I would have enjoyed some different assignments with more specific instructions, like do this sort of thing to accomplish this, or try writing this sort of thing, using this and this. Leaving it as vague as "poetry" and "fiction" was challenging, but I could have used more direction too. I'm not a veteran of creative writing classes, and so therefore I have no defenses built up against the fucked-up things in them as you do. I crave more of the teaching techniques and assumptions of traditional creative writing; I'm not sick of them yet.   Loraine Hutchins

I don't think anyone ever gave me a theory, however practical, that helped me to write better fiction. By this I mean that extended sessions on technique wouldn't be nearly as useful as the study of technique through the analysis of a specific manuscript or published stories.   Valerie Kern

I would have liked more input on the process of writing—not instructions, but sharing talk of basic problems we all must face, instead of plunging directly into the critique.   Dianne Chiddister

As I begin to acknowledge my own problems with self-censorship, I realize that assignments may successfully trigger repressed themes. I also realize that a limited general discussion might ease our intense plunge into focused criticism and strengthen our collective identity as writers. However, I would still make assignments optional and would subordinate general discussion to our critical scrutiny of a woman's work.

Discussion

I remember discussions as lively, incisive, and fun. Our range in age (from 19 to 68), lifestyles, and values guaranteed a complex critical feedback that usually spared us pat responses and occasionally involved us in reflective controversy. I especially appreciated the presence of the older women in the class and anticipated sharing their wisdom. Grace Paley pointed out to some of us that "other mothers" can sometimes teach us more than our own, since these relationships are not burdened by the emotional baggage between biological mothers and daughters. Earlier that summer, Adrienne Rich had read the chapter on "Mothers and Daughters" from her then unpublished *Of Woman Born: Motherhood as Experience and Institution*. We were hungry for open communication between generations, ready to reclaim what had been sacrificed to the enmity and alienation of mothers and daughters forced to exist as rivals in the kingdom of the sons.

Yet, I know that the older women sometimes felt uncomfortable, surrounded by women under forty in a youth culture that has distorted the feminist as a . .n-hating provocateur. Or perhaps the older woman anxiously tried to fit in and prove she was "with it." At the very least, she may have discredited her insight in a culture that doesn't value age. One woman said, "I feel like a kindergartner among college students." This particular person was to contribute some of the most sensible criticism during one entire Workshop. She also fascinated us with stories about women of her generation obtaining contraceptives from Margaret Sanger's clinic and fighting local hospital boards (usually unsuccessfully) for their right to be sterilized. She calmly coped with the bats flying in her cabin; on the last day of classes, she left her husband in a dry motel and marched through the muddy woods to be with us.

In other sessions, few relationships with older women developed so smoothly. For example, at the beginning of one particular Workshop, I scheduled discussion of poems by women who had attended an earlier session. Since they already trusted me, I reasoned, they could comfortably break the ice by presenting their work first. The opening day's discussion centered on a complex poem that involved a lesbian relationship. Immediately after class, a white-haired retired schoolteacher sought me out. She felt "morally outraged" at that day's subject matter and proposed to leave the Workshop. I realized that I could not comfort her with the next day's reading, a poem which explicitly described the insertion of a diaphram. I appealed to her commitment to a group that had traveled so far, had spent a substantial sum of money, and at the very least had seriously disrupted their routine to be with each other. I tried to convey the dignity of each person's attempt to document her reality and our responsibility as listeners. She stayed.

Furthermore, she attended each class meeting, contributing comments that formed a valuable minority perspective. Although wary, she did not abandon us with an aloof silence. This generosity characterized almost every woman at each Workshop. Grace Paley had told us that she opened her classes with the following statement.

> If you're not interested in other people's work, I'm not interested in you . . . You have to be for each other. Grace Paley '76

We rarely needed this reminder.

For the first few days of each Workshop, I was particularly careful to monitor discussion. I clearly established my expectations for a supportive atmosphere where tactlessness or malice would not be tolerated. No one was allowed to state a one-dimensional pejorative reaction to work, since "I hate it," or even "I love it," would leave the writer helpless to evaluate response. Each critical comment had to be supported by specific reasoning. It has always seemed to me that the critic shares the writer's vulnerability, since she puts herself on the line when she analyzes.

Sometimes women hesitated to point out the weaknesses of another woman's work, fearing that their negative feedback would be taken as a lack of support. It is crucial that the writer trust the critic's good will and that the critic understand that shrewd negative comment is at the very least constructive and often exhilarating. To censor one's criticism is a lack of generosity and a gesture of contempt that will keep a writer from developing her finest potential.

> The class expected more, you expected more of me, of my poetry in making negative comments, pinpointing problems. I'm really struck by that because I think that shows real supportiveness, real cooperation. Not pointing those out to me would keep me a weaker writer. Melanie Perish

> There are many so-called writing workshops around this country which are rip-offs. Poets essentially tell people their writing is just fine and take their money; they don't work and they don't care about the lives of their students.
> Something very different is happening in the communities of women's workshops. Here, people take each other seriously to the point of being seriously critical. The friends to whom I show my own work are the friends I know will be tough with me. It's that challenge that enables all of us to go beyond ourselves. It's a tribal challenge.
> In this sense, none of us is alone as long as we have access to that kind of reading, of response, of hearing. This is proving to be the strength of women's culture. Adrienne Rich '76

People must feel free to disagree with each other's analysis, including statements made by the teacher.

> The most valuable thing I got out of the Workshop was permission to take a stand. The first day in class I said something about Sherry's poem. The next person to speak contradicted my statement. I began to retract it–or rather revise it to take into account the new statement. You said, "Don't com-

promise. Our function is not to agree. Don't back down." This permission to take a stand led to the tough, articulate criticism that even quiet women were doing by the end of the second week.   Linda Brown

On one particular occasion, after studying Anne Sexton's *Transformations* and Andrea Dworkin's *Woman Hating,* I was convinced that fairy tales contaminate children's imaginations through their display of sexist stereotypes. Consequently, I objected to the positive reference to fairy tales in a poem whose perspective was clearly identified as feminist. Another woman in the class calmly balanced my position:

Even though the negative things we've said about fairy tales are true, we may be needlessly impaled on this subject. The narrator was simply trying to create a picture of the mother as a warm person. She uses the telling of fairy tales to convey a positive relationship with her mother—that they did have some time alone together.   Mary Scheuhing

Personal Conferences

Each woman met with me privately once each week to discuss her work for about forty-five minutes to an hour. I looked forward to the more leisurely pace outside the classroom where I could give my undistracted attention to one individual at a time. I wanted to connect personally with each participant, to sense how she was doing emotionally as well as artistically in our hectic euphoria.

Furthermore, as a critic, I could respond to each word in a particular passage in order to clarify my feedback, to make sure that the writer understood my comments and my good will even if she disagreed with my critical judgments. Specific questioning about her intentions helped me to respond to her work more sensitively and helped her open up to me as a person she could confide in. The writer must feel comfortable with a teacher as a friendly, compassionate person as well as a tough, articulate critic. Otherwise, time together is wasted in the writer's resisting the teacher's suggestions.

What I didn't understand on the scene was that personal conferences helped break down the hierarchical distances between teacher and student, inevitable in a structured classroom. Whether sitting on a comfortable easy chair by exotic indoor plants or resting on the cool stone porch at Pine Lake, I became simply another woman eager to learn from as well as teach my sisters. My enthusiasm confirmed each woman's individual value, contributing to the self-confidence necessary for her to speak out in her own voice.

While class comments were helpful and important, the personal conferences offered each of us criticism which focused on us as individuals rather than as part of a group. I liked the personal conferences because they were private—on a one-to-one basis—which made me feel important and which made me feel that my work was important. Here I clarified—in a discussion with Beverly—the meaning and danger of writing in code. I don't believe I would have accepted this idea from a group; I would have assumed that they hadn't read my work carefully enough.   Holly Russell

The conferences singled each one of us out for structured, personal attention, thus making a statement that our differences were as valuable as our similarities. I also felt that the conferences made you a part of the community in a way which might otherwise not have been possible. You certainly shared yourself as well as your expertise in class sessions, but in one to one conversations I felt you as one of us, a woman and a writer, without the halo of authority that I might otherwise have been tempted to hang about your head. Sherry Redding

Taking Ourselves Seriously

I have seen women try to sabotage their writing by trivializing their own efforts through apology or boast; either response dilutes the intense confrontation demanded between the writer and her words. More than once, I have been dismayed to see how, in their early letters of expectations to me, strong writers describe themselves as scribblers or dabblers, terms that are belittling and inaccurate.

I am interested in meeting other women who scribble in the night—am wondering how they deal with that facet of themselves. Holly Russell

From the Workshop I hope to meet other women who write, join in some good conversations about writing, and try to find some direction for my own writing to take. Have only dabbled in poems, diary keeping.

Martha Ficklen

Feminine modesty in these cases has been a liability, disguising real talent, obstructing serious commitment. And so in '75, few women thought to bring their typewriters to a two-week writing workshop. The following summer, I explicitly listed typewriters as a required item. I was pleased to see a woman who had traveled from California hauling an IBM Selectric into the Hartwick dorms. By then, some of us were giving ourselves more credit.

Before the Workshop, I passed off my writing as a hobby, something I shared with people who knew me. The Workshop altered this. The incisive criticism and the positive support helped me acknowledge the importance of writing, writing honestly in my life. Calling myself a writer, admitting that it was a significant part of my identity, was one of the hardest things I've done. Melanie Perish

I remember that I was taken seriously, by women I respect, for this writing activity which forms no part of my livelihood or external duties. The attention I was given as a writer demands that I pay equal respect, equal concern, to my own writing. So it can never again be enough to scribble four lines in my journal, jot an image on the back of an envelope, finish a poem and dump it in a drawer. Sherry Redding

As a teacher, I have to insist that people take themselves as seriously as I take them. I must listen with equanimity to accusations of rigidity or hardheartedness, because I know that the greatest contribution I can make is to turn people on to the importance of their writing.

You took us seriously as writers, which helped us to take ourselves and one another seriously. This was one of the real values of the Workshop: that common recognition among ourselves that what we're doing is important. In a sense, it is like "coming out of the closet." Not (in my own life) because my writing was not acknowledged, but because it was not emphasized. It was what I'd do when all the other "important" things were done.

Valerie Kern

> Because we were taking our writing seriously we also had to take ourselves and each other seriously. This business of being taken seriously is very important for women, after several centuries of being trained to excel, succeed, even survive by developing an ability to take everyone else's needs, desires, projects, careers, what have you, as more important than our own.
> Sherry Redding

> As a woman struggling to extricate myself from sexist stereotypes, to reclaim what has been withheld from me, I need to know about other women's lives. I believe in our collective genius and I insist that we struggle, that we support one another in this struggle, to restore our own identities. This determination allows me to hold out indefinitely for what I know women can give.

> You put my vision and style on a clearer course and urged me to try things I had been reluctant to do. What I needed was to be pushed, and you did. The result was much better poetry by the end of the second week—I almost surprised myself.
> Paula Gills

> Having stated your commitment to the experience and then following through with action, you infused the group with a sense of purpose. I think this is important because it left me no "out" in my crisis time. I could never say, "Who cares if I'm writing well; no one's really taking this seriously," or "Everyone's giving 50% and that's only human because other things are going on."
> Melanie Perish

As writers, women have to break through the serious disadvantages imposed on us by a culture that dictates that our sacred and exclusive identity is to serve other people, primarily men or young children.

> For a woman the tragedy of being a facilitator is that the facilitator is a victim. When a woman's life is shaped by other people's needs rather than her own, she's been led to believe that her needs are being fulfilled in the act of accommodating other people . . . And since the time-consuming demands made on her are represented as mainly servile (a little love, a few cookies, some dictation), is it any wonder that a woman puts very little value on her own opinions and ideas?
> It doesn't matter that this is an oversimplified picture of our real lives. Nor does it matter that many women, including myself, can say, "But that's not the case with me." The fact that it is the pattern for many women reveals the general condition of women in our world, and that condition affects me in some way because I am a woman.
> Pat McElligott

We have been trained to lose; "girls give up" is a familiar message, institutionally imprinted on us as early as first grade readers. By high school, we understand well that the successful coquette is the floundering achiever.

> The most important constant of the Workshop, a strong reason why I left with a sense of myself as a writer, was that you thought of us as professionals, and treated us as such. All escape through little-girl, novitiate routes were closed. If I didn't take the Workshop seriously, I wasn't taking myself seriously. If I gave up, I necessarily had to question what my identity as a writer meant to me because I knew what it meant to you. This had interest-

ing ramifications: at home, I was irritated with my cute, but too-small desk. Later, I took my typewriter and poems with me on vacation. *Melanie Perish*

If we are cut off from experiencing or acknowledging our power as women in the world, then we will be unable to record biographically or imaginatively our own strength in our writing.

Your behavior said, in effect, "OK. We're not going to play any female games here. You've chosen to come here and work. That was your decision; now that's your responsibility." From the beginning you treated us as adult persons, not as female cripples. *Clara Jones*

Whether they would regard themselves as feminists or not, most women at the Workshops recognized the penalties imposed on them by a sexist culture, and thrived in an atmosphere of open resistance. Personally, I have usually had leisure, a room of my own, a typewriter, and money to buy stationery supplies. What I didn't always have was faith in my own perceptions, the crucial confidence that what I knew was worth recording. The generosity of my sisters towards each other and towards me, our obvious excitement and acknowledgment of our insight, was the beginning of believing I had something important to say and that committing myself to my work was not a pretentious act of self-deception.

The Workshop helped me to clarify basic things about my life as a writer and now I feel a renewed commitment that I haven't felt since discovering that there was such a thing as a creative writing course. Part of that renewed commitment will be to buy a filing cabinet, lay claim to a room, and hire somebody to come in and watch the baby while I lock myself up with a pen. (There: it's in writing.) I believe more than I ever have that my writing is important. If my vision is vague and illusive, it won't always be. Gradually it will come into focus and what it says will be what I'm about.

Valerie Kern

Too often, in order to be nourished professionally we must be willing to mask our wisdom, perhaps even unconsciously, so that we please rather than disturb the men or male-identified women who are reading and judging our work. In academic institutions, many of us have been irresistibly drawn to sit at the Great Man's feet, basking in his intermittent praise. This was our approved source of artistic pride—to play the part of the protegee, the intellectual version of the dancing girl. Some of us were lucky enough to find a good teacher—usually a man, since women teachers are scarce at most colleges—who genuinely admired our work, who generously, consistently encouraged us. But even then, I wonder what lost messages we never dared to record. In a context where sexist propaganda is accepted as truth, where we are expected to lie, we will never be able to record the stories of our lives accurately. We experience what novelist Joanna Russ, instructor of the '76 Fiction Workshop, called "the censorship that gets to people before they even sit down to write."

Liberating Ourselves From Our Secrets

The fact that our insights are threatening or unacceptable, handicaps us as writers. Since lucidity is necessary to eloquence, and since we may be tempted to dilute or obscure what we are afraid to say directly, our writing will suffer. The means by which a woman is sabotaged vary, although the reasons for sabotage are culturally consistent—under patriarchy, all women pay a price for challenging the company line, whether it's specific retaliation in a personal relationship, trivialization or ridicule by male audiences ("You're too political/angry/narrow-minded/sensitive/paranoid"), or simply the loneliness of being an outsider.

Consequently, we may create obstacles against recording difficult situations.

I've not thought much about dealing with my father, but I find myself framing lines, poems in my head about him. Strangely enough, all of these happen when I'm driving in the car and can't write them down.
Melanie Perish

Some of us with unconscious complicity document our lives as they never actually happened or fail to document our lives as they might have happened. I remember particularly a short story by Pat McElligott that involved a sexual encounter (in the genre Clara Jones dubbed "non-intimate fucking") between a wryly, obedient young woman and a stuffy, older man. Pat presented the story in class before she had completed the ending. Later, she mailed me the finished piece in which the woman ultimately refuses to go to bed with the man. Pat wrote, "Before the Workshop, I would have made her go through with it."

Many of us use obscurity to exclude readers because we are afraid to face what we truly feel or are afraid to reveal these feelings publicly.

Writing has always been important to me as a way of recording for myself those feelings and experiences that I wanted to hide from others.
Clara Jones

Or in our lack of confidence, we allow ourselves to be dominated by the beguiling lyricism of the language.

I haven't trusted my voice, but somehow I didn't even have a voice, so much was it suppressed. My life and experiences weren't valid or important so I had to write from the outside in, which resulted not in the chronicle of the stasis or growth of a person but rather bringing words together and contriving a rational order.
Aldona Middlesworth

Whether our obscurity is an attempt to gain privacy, an unconscious dodge of painful feelings, or a misguided technical frivolity, the result is the same—no one understands what we have said. We've taken no risks as writers; our isolation as women is intact.

I attribute both the cracking of these secret codes and the support sustained by a group of women with potentially clashing egos and ideologies as partly the result of our exposure to *Women and Honor: Some Notes on Lying,* a long prose-poem by Adrienne Rich that we heard live in '75 and on tape in '76.

> That night I had the sense that each woman was, in effect, being asked by Adrienne to be each other's mirrors and sources of strength, to be for each other, in a more conscious way than women had been before. There's always been the half-conscious support of the rueful sisterhood, the kaffeekklatsch, the gossip session relating to men and how to get around them. But as women move out of being reactors to men and into being more autonomous, then a new kind of strength and a new standard of honesty (equivalent to level of seriousness) is required.   Linda Brown

> Adrienne's words were like poignant sewing needles as they stitched patches of women's lives into quilts of comprehension.   Ruth Young

In '75, Adrienne Rich read *Women and Honor: Some Notes on Lying* from a hand-written text that she was then still revising. At the time, I remember my excitement that this woman trusted us enough to read her newest poem in our company. We found the poem provocative and moving in its ruthlessly candid documentation of women's dishonesty under patriarchy, where our many silences and lies, including the open acknowledgment of lesbianism as a valid sexual choice, have kept us from truly knowing one another. Even the townspeople were impressed by what they must surely have considered subversive literature. After the reading, one local woman thoughtfully announced to me, "You've found the Tom Paine of the Women's Movement."

Although we had already understood too well the risks of retaliation or rejection when we expose our feelings, we did not fully understand the costs of our denial.

> In lying to others we end up lying to ourselves. We deny the importance of an event, or a person, and thus deprive ourselves of a part of our lives. Or we use one piece of the past or present to screen out another. Thus we lose faith even with our own lives.
>
> ... Truthfulness has not been considered important for women as long as we have been physically faithful to a man, or chaste.
>   Adrienne Rich, *Women and Honor: Some Notes on Lying*

Now as we grasped the value of telling the truth, we anticipated the gains in collective knowledge and personal insights.

> Women have often felt insane when cleaving to the truth of our experience. Our future depends on the sanity of each of us, and we have a profound stake, beyond the personal, in the project of describing our reality as candidly and fully as we can to each other.
>   Adrienne Rich, *Women and Honor: Some Notes on Lying*

We began to feel that liberation meant telling our secrets, that an accurate recording of our lives was an act of bravery rather than an indiscretion.

Results Immediate and Drastic

This infusion of purpose, sustained over time by a supportive community where taboo topics were openly acknowledged and discussed, often dramatically transformed our work. Essentially, people were willing to crack their secret codes and reveal themselves. Clarity became a crucial value.

The criticism in the Workshop sessions and in conference showed me the necessity of dealing with my greatest flaw: my love for needless ambiguity, my tendency to make elliptical leaps no reader can follow, my lazy choice of the lyrical at the expense of the lucid. My immediate job, the Workshop taught me, is to form a synthesis of lyrical lucidity so that even my darkest images cast a clear shadow. Sherry Redding

"Breakthrough" poems written during the Workshop or immediately afterwards were a drastic contrast between new and old work. At least one participant attributed this contrast to the fact that women may intentionally hold back their best writing until they have investigated the critical climate.

It is possible that the poetry submitted to you in the mail is sent tentatively, that it is no-risk poetry, and that after finding out that you do indeed treat the work carefully, then, and only then, do people come out with their real goodies. This is not to say there is not growth during the Workshop because I believe there truly is; space is provided and experiences occur that people want to work out. But I do believe that some of the diversity you discovered between the first series of poems and the second series of poems owes itself to the trust element, to the tremendous consideration you show a poem, and to the care with which you treat the revelations of each writer. Nancy Osborne

Although I acknowledge the reluctance of people to share their most intimate work immediately, I must disagree with this statement, if only for the fact that too often writers do not know what their best work is and therefore cannot deliberately withhold it. I feel that the dramatic transformation of work is the result of a political climate generated by a feminist writing community. When women believe they have valuable things to say that will be responsibly received, they become intent on accurately depicting their experience instead of tempering, disguising, or avoiding their insight altogether.

I now use the Workshop as a lodestar. Up to the Workshop, many poems of mine were totally inaccessible —unclear because I thought what I was saying didn't merit intelligibility. So instead of using words as tools to express meaning, I hid behind them and used them for their own sake. Now when I sit at my desk and start to write such a poem I recall Bev's admonitions and the group's support and confirmation of me as a woman and as a writer with valuable things to say and I feel less fearful and can more easily come to clarity. In other words, I trust my voice more. Aldona Middlesworth

This commitment to clarity may mean we are willing to write about new subjects or more shrewdly evaluate current themes. Often a magnanimous, socially approved narrative voice will shift into a more honest, explicitly accusing perspective, as in Dianne Chiddister's before and after poems. In Holly Russell's and Mary Ann Scheuhing's work, the more generalized doom of the earlier poems tightens to the detailed, accessible grievances of the later work. The defiant tone and the unconventional stands in the the work of Dale Darling and Barbara Bickel, then Hartwick students, significantly differ from the poems of the typical undergraduate at a small conservative college. Aldona Middlesworth clears the gorgeous density and reveals herself.

Barbara Bickel

I was promised
    a balcony on the beach
    moonlight parties
    eternal sunshine
for
    nights of acrobatics
    award-winning groans
    energetic faking
I chose cold weather

I was sent
    love notes under my door
    flowers on right occasions
    "nothing special" bracelets
for
    evenings of groping
    feigned passion
    boredom
I changed my address

I had
    long talks of Sartre and Camus
    stale wine and sour cheese
    endless walks in early morning dusk
for
    a rootless tongue
    scratchy beard
    rough hands
I said I was a virgin

Dale Darling
Evolution: Then and Now

Somewhere the blacksmith
forges out the male mystery code
on the anvil shaped like
a woman's head.

And that same woman
sits and churns the butter
that he spreads on his bread.

But now we remember that
Aphrodite choked
on Eros' kisses

And Joan of Arc
did not wear
a chastity belt

And Sappho
did not own a dildo.

Breakthrough Poems

The following poems are paired chronologically. Each writer arrived at the Workshops with the first poem and wrote the second poem during our time together or shortly afterwards.

Holly Russell

    trapped—

i am too subjective

calloused on the wrong surfaces

my mind flies by carrying all
that is crucial—all
that is not lonely.

grasping their hands,
        eyes,

   i wheel and smile,
   wring these insides out.

i am coping
but not surviving.

Nana

Nearing the end
when you saved the feet of chickens
you'd killed for our dinner
in jars on a shelf,
my aunt told me not to mind you—
"Old age is difficult for some women."
Even at eight,
I couldn't accept that—
Then you were gone.

She betrayed you, Nana, as I watched
from the door of your bedroom—
she lowered your dresses and shoes into a box
to give to the poor,
laid pieces of you—a rhinestone barrette, a brooch, a stocking—
on the bed,
discarded them like trinkets
from some man
whose face she'd forgotten.
Fearful and angry, I mouthed a sound—a shout—
"Leave them alone;
she'll come back for what's hers"
and ran from the room
that still smelled like death.

Nana, I do not believe that love exists
outside of the movies
or that trust is more than hope
for love—
I count my friends like used matchsticks in a row—
I count my aunt traitor—
Your name is a scar on my cheek;
like blood, your madness leaks from my mouth—

Obsessed with you
who have gone beyond listening
I count your death in tens,
walk toward your sleep like a specter,
      a stranger in every house.

Holly Russell's After Statement

I have always written out my thoughts and ideas on the nearest little slip of paper I could find. My words found a place on the backs of lists, on used envelopes, on the undersides of countless wrappers. Because my thoughts flow uncontrollably when I'm driving a car (the movement itself is inspiring!), I've written pages of notes to myself with a pen in one hand and the steering wheel in the other. My car has been continually cluttered with little torn-up pieces of paper, covered with the scribbles that record my life.

Until the Women's Writing Workshop, it never occurred to me that there was anything strange or significant about this method. It is clear to me now that the method itself is a statement which says that only when I am moving from one place to another am I free to express my moods and needs without interruption. Only as a "woman driving alone" am I so involved in myself that I can spew forth the words that are so necessary for my survival. Here I will record all I have learned and all I do not know—and I will risk my life (and the lives of those around me) to do so. The little slips of paper—easily lost or discarded—say something else as well: these words are only important when they touch the page; from then on they deserve no respect.

I am relieved to voice the confessions these statements hold, though I admit I still occasionally write while driving. Perhaps I haven't yet faced the whole truth in the method itself. But my attitude has changed. Now the little torn-up bits covered with ink and lead have become gold, and all are carefully placed in labelled envelopes for later use as poems or parts of poems.

Diane Chiddister

Together

The bleeding never stops.

Blood passes between us, the soft flow turns
    metal hard, a chain of wounds.
Wounds which sleep together, wounds which understand
    each other's suffering.
    Reason to stay.
And the bed lingers red.

We lacerate each other
    with all that we are not.
Bound in sheets, skins scraping, we touch
        and break into glass statues which
           bend and flow and come together, slowly.

You never let me hold you in your sleep.
You consume too much air.
I gasp for breath, choking
on my own slow need.

Together (Revised)

You say
my blood is red
as a wounded whore.

You tell me
I fuck hard as horses.
Bound in sheets
skins scraping
you ride me.
Ride me.
I gush with noise.

Your back is turned away
and locked.
You dream of virgins.
I lie awake
and stain the bed.

Interview With Dianne Chiddister on Her Revision of "Together"

BT: Why is the revision so much more explicit than the original poem?

DC: In rewriting "Together" it was important for me to go back and re-experience my feelings. The poem couldn't be clear to anybody else until it was clear to me. Writing the second poem was a kind of catharsis.

BT: When you presented the original poem to the class, did you think it was clear? Why did you decide to revise? Did the class discussion trigger something in you?

DC: I obviously wasn't getting my message across; I mean people didn't know what I was talking about. The feeling of the writer—or the feeling of the narrator—wasn't clear. That was the main thing.

BT: And you accepted that.

DC: Yeah.

BT: You accepted the validity of the feedback.

DC: I knew I trusted the women in class. I wasn't satisfied with that poem. It was a matter of not really *knowing* how to be more clear, or how to go back and take the experience and turn it into something that other people really could feel.

BT: But I'm still impressed with the fact that the revision amounts to an emotional and artistic breakthrough. When people explain to me that my poem is not clear, I don't necessarily know how to fix it. It's an impressive thing to me—as another poet and as a teacher—that the "corrections" you made overnight boomed through to your meaning. They're extremely successful revisions.

DC: That's very exciting. I tried to go back to the situation and to re-experience it. And I said to myself, "O.K., in the simplest way possible, what are you feeling?"

BT: But in the revision, the experience not only becomes more clear, but actually changes. In class, people criticized the inconsistency of your imagery—the jump from blood to metal to glass. But most people accepted the philosophical attitudes. The first two stanzas seemed to be acknowledgment of mutual pain in a sexual context. Although I don't think we determined the gender of the people involved, it was clearly a sexual situation depicted by a just voice: "I hurt you, you hurt me; no one is to blame." A few women objected to the accusation in the last stanza as inconsistent with the earlier magnanimity.

I had the feeling you were going to rewrite the glass imagery, because there was a lot of controversy on that. But then your revision evolved as a powerful, coherent statement of accusation. The whole emotional point of view changed.

DC: Well, in the first poem I talked about the relationship being destructive and hurting in pretty general kinds of ways. I needed to go back and clarify my own pain, to confront how a particular person had hurt me.

BT: At first you were recording the consequence of that hurt, not the origin. "This is how it feels to be hurt" rather than "Why do I feel hurt?"

DC: Yeah.

BT: "You tell me / I fuck hard as horses" are very shocking lines for me. Those words give me a sense of the abuse from the other person, of a kind of shame trip that's being put on the narrator. Explain how you got that out of the original poem. Why did "Together" evolve from the "We all hurt each other" to explicit accusation and documentation of pain?

DC: No one actually told me I fuck like horses, but "hard" was applied to me. I was told that I fucked really hard, which was not a nice thing. I didn't like that at all; that sounded really awful. And the "as horses" was added on to convey the brutality of that description. That horse image was the best one I could think of to show how repulsive I was made to feel.

BT: Why didn't you say that in the first poem? And what allowed you to say it in the second one?

DC: I felt more aware of my own feelings, of being exploited. The thing that I think happens to a lot of women is feeling from a man that you're a dirty, repulsive woman if you are able to be sexually free. And at the same time that man is taking your sexuality and using it and enjoying it but putting you down for it. Sometimes it's hard to see that's happening. You're not quite sure what's going on, but it sure doesn't feel good. I think a lot of people have experienced that. I think it's easy to identify with.

BT: Earlier we said that you were able to write a vulnerable, artistically powerful statement because you felt that other women would understand, that your poem wouldn't be treated as an exposé of your own isolated, neurotic experience. Do you think this was possible because you were with other women here?

DC: Definitely. Hearing other women be so open in their own poems made me feel like I could say anything. The experience in "Together" would have been pretty hard to bring in the first day and talk about. But other people really took a lot of risks with things they were saying. So I felt that, at least in this group, I could take risks, too.

BT: How do you think men would have reacted to "You dream of virgins. / I lie awake / and stain the bed"? How would you have felt about presenting that to a class of men?

DC: Really uncomfortable. Though I think certain men could learn something from that, they would have had a hard time accepting it. They would feel too threatened. Because I think it's something many men do, and they're really not aware that they're doing it, even though they do it.

BT: Men might punish you for your insight.

DC: I would probably fear that that would happen.

BT: Have you showed this revision to the women here?

DC: Yeah, I showed it to a couple of them.

BT: What's their reaction?

DC: They really liked it. I felt their support.

Mary Ann Scheuhing

An Imagination on the Genetics of Suicide

Today, mother,
the anniversary of mourning,
no change is in the grieving
only ever better understood.
I sense surreal biology
your acid strands uncoiled in me
helices of disillusion
the older sadder being
replicating misery in my youth,
doublest helix of despair.

Protean memory of you lingers
in February cakes and valentines
in perfumed thighs and dry
but willing breasts
a silhouette beside a stove
a bowl of plain oatmeal
a box of green gummed stars
small cinnamon potatoes
from an Irish candy store in March
numbness twice relieved by pain.

Code words reach me faintly
I strain to overhear
the loving sound of some
shooting through my cells
urging proper pairing
for the synthesis of hope.
But the message is ill transcribed
a transfer somewhere fails,
nucleotide muddle.

No worthy codon
makes the journey now
through the viscous ground
of daughter cells;
words for laughter
are lost in the dark,
sentences for death are not
and coming blurred
they threaten me
more and more numerous
out of the templates
nearer the ribosome seat.
But I resist
and block the exhortation
with all my neutralizing chemical
refuse to read it out.

Recollections of My Mother

#1   Loss

My seven years against your forty-nine,
we sat at the kitchen table
amid the cloudy glasses, rings of milk
a butter smudge, cereal toys,
toast crumbs welded to a jellied knife.
I tried not to scratch the prickly heat
blazing a shield on my chest;
I pressed for cool against the metal table.

> Here the film is spliced,
> the tape erased.
> I angered you
> some crime of disrespect
> that smashed a summer day
> that sent the month of June
> electric shocking through
> my brain.

You left the house.
"I am never coming back,"
you said that.
I called to you,
your thin spine receding,
warping in my view
through tears, and screen and sun.
A last triangle of your shirt
disappeared around the corner.
I vomited saltines and peaches.
I ran for you; it had to be a game.
I skimmed the streets and stores,
mistaking other women for my mother.

You did return, to find me waiting
inside the thought of your perfume,
with the taste of your blouse in my mouth
and the stripes of your skirt
permanent bars across my eyes.

Aldona Middlesworth

He sits in a kaleidoscope
of art, that he hawks

bit by variegated bit.
Bourbon in the meadow grass

of a china bull stomach
nips his hand flaskness.

He assesses years by

cartwheels in steeple-

chases. Two ago
he was muffing coke

and bungling acid.
Shapeless expeditions

into a mirror.
Trailed by girls,

draped with entrails,
workings (of his face)

would surface, then
explode, internal

holocaust. Flame away,
and out into

dark corridors where
tap dancers

heel by toe by.
Gloam, crystal angles,

gloam. For him,
offal is girder.

One year ago,
such flips,

smoking rope
thickened him

to skinned pudding
no center or surface

for bolster. Only drays
for formality's sake.

Like schizophrenia
his days were jelled

nebular, by
festoons of sun paranoia.

He covered his slots
as he walked.

Now he slumps
over a lofty shelf

where bottles in a series
still stand.

He is fortified limp
liquid. Flotation has

no need to dilate
prism skin.

Instructions on how to sell roses in the fine restaurants, to the gentlemen for their ladies

You must first present a picture—
you, standing at the edge of the dining room.
A girl in a white blouse, soft skirt,
red roses in a straw basket under her arm.

While presenting this old-fashioned snapshot
of someone who used to be,
you must seem to loll.
But you must not be idle.

Instead you must probe the room
for your first customer.
Likely ones are
a young man with a young girl
an old man with a young girl
or an affluent-looking man
(In this case, the age of the female
is irrelevant—just as he imagined
you're someone you're not
he will imagine
she's someone she's not).

You now approach the table
you've chosen.
Be certain to smile at the woman first
or else she'll be jealous at your intrusion.
Nestle yourself between them.
Bend down
so your eyes are level with theirs.
Place the basket of roses
quite near her nose.
Lift out one full-blown
and present it to him
as if it's a trophy
for one of his important achievements.
Slowly rotate your head to her.
Then ask if the gentleman would like
to buy a rose for the lady tonight.

You can immediately sense a no
by her strong eyes
which refuse to believe
she's someone she's not.

Towards the New Feminist Ethic

Although we gloried in our insight, we also discussed the difference between progaganda and art in order to avoid a forced ideology that can swamp the best-intentioned efforts. We were unwilling to confuse politically correct rhetoric with eloquence or to record as awesome events mere bandwagon miracles. For example, one woman presented a poem praising a man who was willing to help his lover insert her diaphragm. Immediately, another woman challenged the narrator's admiration because the man's gesture was superficial in that restricted context of the bedroom. Another time, a woman attempted to write a poem from an essentially female spiritual perspective. She was closely questioned on the accuracy of each reference to matriarchal deities.

No one got away with holding up flashcards of WOMAN, RIVER, MOON, CIRCLE. You in particular and the group as a whole always asked what this meant, was this an authentic experience.   Sherry Redding

In this context of attentive critical inquiry, we attempted to render into powerful artistic statement the political insights that have changed our lives.

I believe that lives get affected and changed by writing. We are what we read. The content of literature really does affect how we perceive ourselves, how we think we have to make our choices, how we think we have to live our lives. The solution is not to have a literature full of strong women, self-affirming: that would be another kind of propaganda. But there has to be some complex way of showing what we know is true—that throughout history, women have had enormous strength, women have affirmed and supported each other; women have not been the eternal losers and victims. Though overall the oppression has been enormous.   Adrienne Rich '76

This stereotype of women as "the eternal losers and victims" made some of us feel most legitimate documenting our distress.

Poetry is in the realm of desperation and/or lust and love. I wonder now if my poems don't have the edge of desperation whether they're worth keeping.   Alice Walker '76

Women have power whether we choose to use it or not, as I've written in the poem "Power." The fight to withdraw from that power has been terribly damaging.   Audre Lorde '77

Yet, at the same time, we did not want to censor our pain by confusing it with self-defeat. At the Pine Lake Workshop in '76, Audre Lorde's reading of her poem "Power" conveyed anger as judgment rather than capitulation, by documenting the breakdown of compassion and justice and the social consequences of that breakdown. In making clear that lack of political consciousness becomes complicity, "Power" inspires, demands that each of us acknowledge our responsibilities in being morally accountable to one another.

Audre Lorde

Power

The difference between poetry and rhetoric
is being ready to kill
yourself
instead of your children.

I am trapped on a desert of raw gunshot wounds
and a dead child dragging his shattered black
face off the edge of my sleep
blood from his punctured cheeks and shoulders
is the only liquid for miles
and my stomach
churns at the imagined taste while
my mouth splits into dry lips
without loyalty or reason
thirsting for the wetness of his blood
as it sinks into the whiteness
of the desert where I am lost
without imagery or magic
trying to make power out of hatred and destruction
trying to heal my dying son with kisses
only the sun will bleach his bones quicker.

A policeman who shot down a ten year old in Queens
stood over the boy with his cop shoes in childish blood
and a voice said "Die you little motherfucker" and
there are tapes to prove it. At his trial
this policeman said in his own defense
"I didn't notice the size nor nothing else
only the colour". And
there are tapes to prove that, too.

Today that 37 year old white man
with 13 years of police forcing
was set free
by eleven white men who said they were satisfied
justice had been done
and one Black Woman who said
"They convinced me" meaning
they had dragged her 4'10" Black Woman's frame
over the hot coals
of four centuries of white male approval
until she let go
the first real power she ever had
and lined her own womb with cement
to make a graveyard for our children.

I have not been able to touch the destruction
within me.
But unless I learn to use
the difference between poetry and rhetoric
my power too will run corrupt as poisonous mold
or lie limp and useless as an unconnected wire
and one day I will take my teenaged plug
and connect it to the nearest socket
raping an 85 year old white woman
who is somebody's mother
and as I beat her senseless and set a torch to her bed
a greek chorus will be singing in 3/4 time
"Poor thing. She never hurt a soul. What beasts they are."

Audre Lorde's After Statement

BT: For the new feminist ethic, we need rules that are moral and humane, and we have to work these out collectively. In "Power" you take responsibility as a woman and judge another woman within a context of absolute compassion.

AL: We have a function, not only with ourselves and with each other, but with the world. It's not an external responsibility; it's a responsibility that flows in the same way that our blood flows, that our juices flow.

Adrienne Rich, Audre Lorde, and Alice Walker all read us portions of their work where the courageous documentation of pain in a sexual context resulted in greater power for the women speaking. Since they better understood the implications and consequences of their lovemaking, they were less apt to victimize themselves or other women through their sexual choices. These writers depicted an ethic of responsibility in sexual relationships.

In Alice Walker's novel *Meridian* the main character refuses to include lovemaking in her longtime friendship with a man who has seriously disappointed her.

It wasn't just that Truman had mistreated Meridian in a sexual way but that as long as he was refusing his responsibility to another woman, she would not have sex with him.
Until we do that for each other, we are all sunk.
Because if a man, for example, has mistreated or abandoned his children or his wife, and if he would come cross town and into your house and you invite him eagerly into your bed and into your life, what in the world are we fighting for?
Alice Walker '76

Adrienne Rich's *From an Old House in America* codifies this sexual discrimination, this link between the ethical and erotic.

A dream of tenderness

wrestles with all I know of history
I cannot now lie down

> with a man who fears my power
> or reaches for me as for death
>
> or with a lover who imagines
> we are not in danger

Who you sleep with—whether male or female—is a political act in the sense that a sexual confirmation implies an endorsement of the "mind that lives in (the) body"* you are loving.

Audre Lorde, in an interracial context, counsels that erotic love between women can begin as consolation for shared political oppression. However, this sexual pleasure must become a lifesource as powerful as the oppressor's threat of death.

> you will be white fury in my navel
> I will be your night
> Mawulisa foretells our bodies
> as our hands touch and learn from each other's hurt . . .
>
> we have always been sisters in pain . . .
>
> women exchanging blood
> in the innermost rooms of moment
> we must taste of each other's fruit
> at least once
> before we shall both be slain.
>
> Audre Lorde in "Meet"**

---

*Adrienne Rich, "Splittings," *Amazon Quarterly* 3, no. 2 (March 1975): 22.

**Audre Lorde, "Meet," in *Snail Shells From the Dooryard of King Toggah*, unpublished manuscript, 1976.

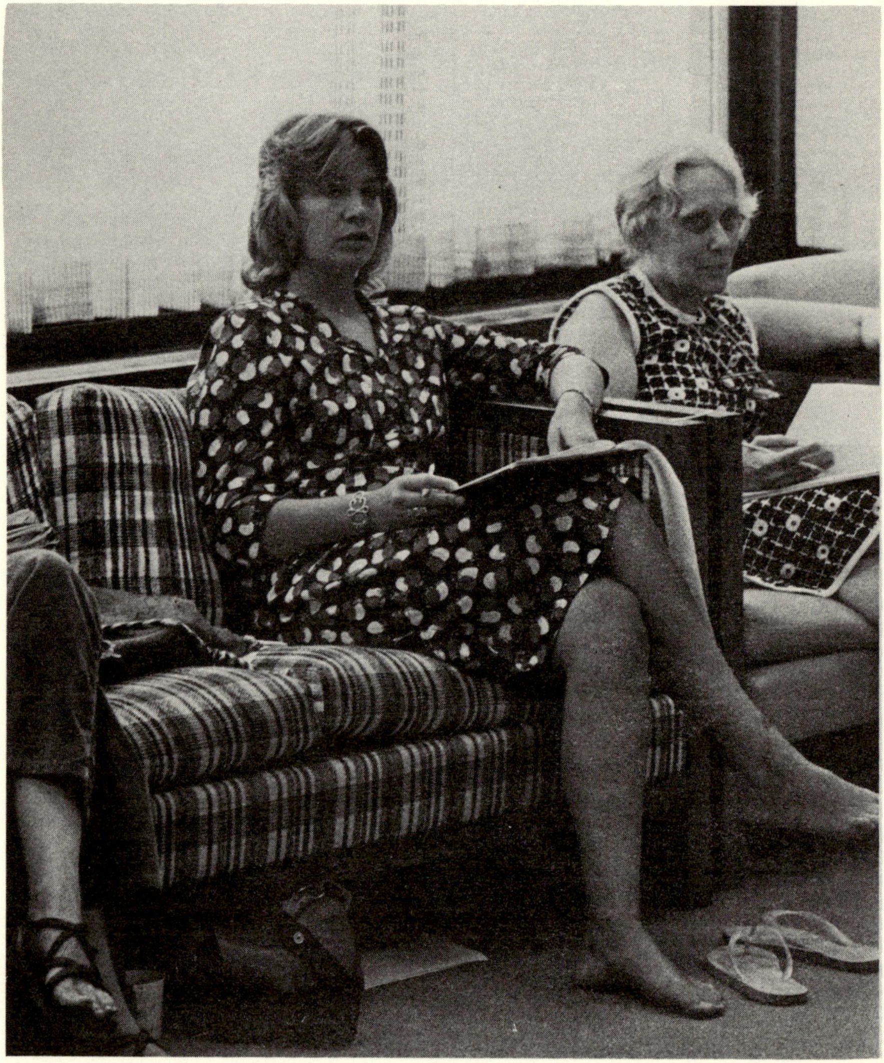

Within the Workshops, participants shared insights about their own sexual experiences, their own struggles to evolve new moral choices.

Melanie Perish

Turning Away

A year ago you would have been
a conquest,
something I had to have
to have myself.

An active listener,
I would have won you:
my wry smile turning gentle,
my graceful shoulder leaning in, intense.
I was adept with the well-placed pause,
the appropriate falter
before the sentence that stated
your sensitive confusion.

Wanting your hands
I'd understand you in return
for the palm that cupped
my breast to your mouth,
the fingers that wandered my thighs,
but in that quilt-safe comfort
acceptance would mark my loss.

Today
after the lecture you stop me,
tell me I think like a man
as your eyes beckon.
I say that this is no compliment
as you bend to light my cigarette;
No
You're glad to be my colleague,
You say I make you think—
and smiling I turn away,
choosing not to listen, to speak or understand,
not even for the touch
of your sandy hair.

Beverly Tanenhaus

The Indulgence of Love

> "Any woman who wants to have the praise
> of the world, must indulge in love."
> Andreas Capellanus, 1186

> "Yet never have we been closer to the truth
> of the lies we were living."
> Adrienne Rich, 1971

And so I told you
about him.
That first time—
the snap of the locked door—
sudden familiarity
of hair, skin,
the movements of his tongue.

I wanted you
to believe
I was still like you:
a woman hungry
for a man's touch.
"You don't think any marriage can last," you said.
"No man is good enough for you."
And I knew you guessed
that what I envied about your wedding
were your gifts.

So I admitted
the weight of him above me
on the rug, his arms
around my shoulders.
I told you I dreamt that
always my body would float
along those hands.

As proof,
I spilled each detail
I didn't want to tell.
The witty letters,
expensive airplanes, double beds,
anguished accusations:
his wife wouldn't dust; his children made too much noise.
An older man,
he lived in a secluded beachfront house,
accustomed to a willed tranquility:
the muted echo of a fog horn,
the pantomime of ocean outside his door.

2.
Eventually I frightened him.
I do not like to dust and I make noise.
A pretty flower that opened once,
I became pressed into a memory.
Such things have tiny lifespans.

I tell you
I do not think
he misses me.
I tell you
I grieve
for him.

You remember
that you met him once.
His charming indirection
pleased you.
"But maddening in an affair," you say.
"It means he doesn't answer questions."

My forgery
has appeased you.
You believe we share the twinned identities
of women who value our lives
by the men who love us.

I have not told you
that sometimes his hands
fluttered like creatures
dying on my body.
Fragile as blown glass
I couldn't cry out
or I would shatter,
cutting him to pieces.

Mornings his children
laughed, getting ready for school.
In the guest room
I pretended to be asleep,
ashamed to admit I was awake.

I promise you
I will grieve for him
but I am lying.
He was a man who thought I was a flower.
I was a woman who faked transparency,
dangerous as glass.

The prince's hands
turn into magical beasts;
the kiss of the prince
makes me come alive.
These things no longer interest me.
          3.
I am a woman rising into my body.
I do not understand yet what this means.

But I promise
I will no longer
lie for you.

Linda Brown

Gathering a Self

When I was ten
I slept outdoors
in a cotton bag
under Colorado stars,
outline of pine.
At Girl Scout camp
we led mules
& bathed in mountain streams
so cold they froze
your period.
I dreamed of my counselor Di.

A poem is a field
of wheat under moonlight.
I have hiked
a long long time
& as I walked I planted
each silver spear.
As day comes
absent of metaphor
I have a field
I have a harvest

There were chairs
of rock in that
mountain stream
we sat on like queens.
The water was a shock
at midday
between our young
thin thighs.
I've never left
Girl Scout camp.
The world: a forest of women
with bushy thighs
and legs that bend
          downstream
         burn like water
at high altitude.

I know now she was a dyke.
my swimming instructor
at Colorado Women's College
who drove a large bike
("faster in traffic")
wore a thick leather jacket
made us kick endlessly
at the edge of the pool

until our legs grew strong.
In a love poem to women,
begin with her.

The bed
in my friends' apartment
is bending.   It squeaks concentration.
Silence is different when love
is being made.   Made
out of nothing.
                    Silence warps
like wind pushing down prairies
& everything catches fire.
                    I made love today—
felt strong as a volcano
                    all that lava
pouring inward
gathering   toward my core
my hands are   gathering
at the fire pit of my vulva
body insistent intent
moving up   and down
grain elevator
stacking silos full
of golden moans
mouths open
like furrows in the earth.

It snowed tonight in San Diego.
first time in nine years.
Snow on the desert floor
icing on telephone wires
that shout uninterrupted
into blackness where stars sizzle.
My friend lived in the desert
for a year   reading Jung in her trailer
riding horseback on hot afternoons.
Lived alone   in a town of 2000:
I could not have done that.
In her desert year   she asked
to make love to me
My flesh stood on end
ladders of open mouths
hungry for honey,
hosanna of tongues.
I said no.
This is what a snowfall is
the crying of all those mouths.

unlearning & unclothing
    where i have been the fog burns off
    ocean shows her skin
unlearning & unclothing
    to be naked
    with myself
husks fall like skirts   the seed
rooted   begins its turn
    in earth   its pirouette
    toward light

Conflict

The significant expenditure of time, money, and travel usually implies that each woman has seriously deliberated her choice to attend the Workshops; once on the scene, she has a vested interest in the program's success.

Fill me. Give me everything you can. Demand that I do the same. I want to walk out of here different from the woman who walked in. Paula Gills

I also knew that the Workshop would be the centerpiece of my year and would determine what I would do creatively for the rest of it. Pat McElligott

A Workshop participant may experience disappointment as a significant loss both financially and spiritually. All of us have had to give up something to get here, and there are no guarantees that the Workshops will repay our efforts. As women, our mobility is often limited by family commitments in a culture that regards time spent away from home in the company of other women as a frivolous or hostile act. For any one of us, joining a group of strangers collectively identified as writers requires a bravery and self-confidence hard to sustain in a culture that trivializes our achievements and conspires against our independence.

In any new community there are fears, loneliness, at being away from friends and lovers, anxieties before new friends are made, and perhaps identity crises about being a writer. Those first three days are often a lonely period when I wonder if I will be able to break through and communicate to anyone in the group. Linda Brown

For many of us in the Workshop, deciding to come and coming was a major political step, made even more significant because it was so closely associated with our personal identities and the work we had made a commitment to. Clara Jones

My decision to attend the Workshop was tantamount to a commitment to write and to define myself from that point on primarily as a writer.
Pat McElligott

The Workshops eliminate the traditional criteria for admissions. On a first come, first served basis, women are accepted into the program on their own say-so.

By applying, we labeled ourselves writers, and you took our word for it. This is very important for women writers, it seems to me, since we are so seldom accepted at our own valuation. Kay Tipsord

On the other hand, despite detailed preliminary information to Workshop participants, the lack of an official selection process results in an occasional mismatching. The discrepancies in artistic and critical sophistication from participant to participant are less problematic than individual adjustments to the highly-charged emotional atmosphere. Each session, a few women may choose to leave early.* I do not interfere with these decisions, honor-

---

*In '75, 3 out of 25 women left. In '76, 1 out of 20 women left my Poetry Workshop; 3 out of 17 left the Fiction Workshop.

ing the autonomy of individuals, and realizing that the other side of exhilaration is anxiety—at the onslaught of controversies and demands that unsettle familiar positions.

And Adrienne, in talking about honesty, really hit on the key; honest enough to admit that you feel lonely, that you need support; honest enough to tell a woman the truth about her work and life, believing in her strength to change. Linda Brown

Yet some women did not experience this honesty as a gesture of affirmation but rather as an uncomfortable, forced exposure.

I refuse to insist that women can always heal each other's wounds. Occasionally, someone will write to me, long after the trauma of early departure.

It is 4:30 a.m. this Friday morning, January 7, and I suddenly want more than anything in the world to communicate with you and tell you how much the Workshop meant to me. Pat Argue

Once we realize the cost of our past isolation and our value as a mutual resource, we may become overzealous. Craving each other's company, we may actually crowd one another.

People were not, by the way, nearly that careless of my time. But it's still a very difficult situation when the woman who drives you to the supermarket will suddenly say, "By the way, what did you think of my story?" You think, "Oh, Jesus, I've got to be tactful and constructive and listen, and all that. Not again. Not now." Joanna Russ '76

In '75, it did not strike me as overly taxing to participants for classes to be extended from the scheduled 2 hours an extra ½ hour each day and to congregate on Saturday and Sunday. It seemed we couldn't get enough of each other. One woman had to get a prescription for sleeping pills since she resisted sleep as a waste of time when she could be either writing or talking with other women. We regarded each other as a critical source of nourishment, destined to disappear in a matter of days.

Yet our enthusiasm for each other at times lapsed into desperation.

I knew I had so much to learn from the people there that I was continually in the role of open receiver, taking in much more than I could handle, not forcing myself away to critically perceive or think through a fraction of what I was being exposed to. This hit an all-time low by Saturday of the first week. At that point I simply did not know what I thought. Melanie Perish

I'm thinking primarily of ways to mellow some of the intensity of that first week. I loved it, but some of us got a little strung out. If we knew that we had a longer time period together, perhaps we wouldn't start with the feeling that this was our chance and it all had to be said and done as soon as possible. Sherry Redding

Unfortunately, I had grandly proclaimed at our opening dinner in '75 that two weeks was clearly an insufficient space. I might just as well have blown a whistle; our race had begun. Although in '76 at both sessions, I deliberately played down our limited time span and repeatedly reassured people that friendships would continue after we had left, we were plagued, to varying degrees, by this same intensity.

I left because I felt exhausted mentally, physically, and spiritually—it got to a point where I could barely think—there was too much to think.
Carol Gargan

For future Workshops, perhaps applicants should be warned of the acute level of emotional stress.   Melissa Wills

I know now that it is crucial not to over-schedule the Workshops, that two overnight visiting writers are plenty, that a feminist press editor should be scheduled on a weekend when there are no classes, that despite my obsessive character and the enthusiastic lobbying of participants, classes must not run over 2½ hours a day, and week-ends are a necessary free space.

At first I was disappointed that for the most part only two hours per day were formally scheduled for classes, but after a few days I was grateful—a heavier load would have been too much for me for more than a week.
Jennifer Kilpatrick

Nonetheless, our stay in an all women's community is limited; our re-entry into culture that daily undermines our competence and self-esteem is inevitable. We may anxiously solicit each other's insight and support; we may feel frustrated or angry if we sense that anyone is holding back.

I think women's community has more potential for creativity and for destructiveness than mixed community. I think the reason it's more volatile for me personally is that I expect more of women than of men. Linda Brown

Maybe in feminism one goes from feeling that women are simply allies and that relationships with them are simple (compared with what one faces with men) to a stage in which the fact that women matter *means that relationships with men become simple and easy (because they don't really count) and relationships with women become horribly problematic and important.*   Joanna Russ '76

Of course the key to the whole thing, this year as last, was simply the meeting of women from all over the country who had so much in common. It makes the whole experience a continuing one, since we will keep in touch with at least some of those women. It makes the whole thing much more emotional, too, which is obviously why some of the women who came had to leave, and why there were conflicts and arguments. But all those things seem to me to be healthy signs that nobody here is just going through motions, that everyone is involved, and has made a personal commitment of some kind.   Kay Tipsord

But it is just this intense personal commitment that makes the stakes so high for us. Because we know how much we need and how little the culture at large can give us, we may distort the significance of our own interactions. As the most visible person in charge, I feel particularly vulnerable to criticism. I've convened the occasion and am saddled with responsibilities, projected by participants or self-imposed. Like many women, I am not entirely comfortable as a leader, occasionally feeling my power to be illusory or illegitimate. Sometimes I feel guilty that I'm in charge, even though I trust my expertise and believe that order is essential for coherence. This makes me especially sensitive to the few complaints at each Workshop that a structured classroom is anti-feminist, that all decisions—including the increase of classes from 2 to 3 hours a day—should be decided by majority vote.

The whole idea that you can destroy structure with chaos is ridiculous. Out of chaos has come mistakes.

What we are trying to develop is non-oppressive structures. There's a difference between a lack of structure and a non-oppressive structure. People very frequently don't realize this. Sometimes I've spent a whole workshop discussing what rules are possible, the reasons for them, how they function. There are certain things that work and certain things that don't.
                                                                   Audre Lorde '77

Occasionally a woman will enter the program who does not take her writing seriously. She may resist criticism, misconstruing critical judgment as overly intellectual or anti-feminist. In a large class, this problem is self-correcting; she will be caught up by the class's determination and excitement. In a small group, she can command more attention, at times plunging us into needless debate over procedure. Or she may try to transform class time into a more informal session, where we uncritically swap life stories.

Any woman who leads a workshop must come to terms with the real power generated by her position. Then she can deal more sensitively with students, freed from her needless fears of being discredited by them. I discussed this particular issue with Audre Lorde.

BT: *I have to acknowledge my power at the Workshops. Then I wouldn't get so undone at personal challenges to my authority. As a woman, it's difficult since I have had power so seldom in my life or had so little opportunity to acknowledge my power.*

AL: *But you have to remember that having power doesn't mean that you're not going to be afraid. A power position is one where you can feel the threat and know that you can handle it.*

At each Workshop there is always one person—usually no more—who wants to take over. By needling at the format through contesting rules as authoritarian, anti-feminist, or as simply not valuable, she tries to re-vamp the program.

Women want power themselves and yet are ready to punish any woman who breaks the feminine taboo of winning. For all our talk of collectivity, we still have to learn that power grows by being shared, that personal power can be infinite. Within a group, every woman can be forceful instead of there being only one, as seen as the leader, who must be challenged.
                                                                   Sherry Redding

Because this competition is usually elevated as an ideological conflict, we are unable to ackowledge openly the power struggle oppressing both of us. I try to defuse the antagonism between us through an unflagging courtesy in class and through a personal appeal in private where I simply tell her that I feel badly that we're not getting along, that I regret our anger and would like to work things out. As a teacher, I know the importance of trusting the group to veto unreasonable suggestions by a single participant.

You have to understand why competition is predictable and what it comes out of in order to deal with it so it doesn't become only a personal vendetta. You musn't see this as an attack on you; it's an attack on authority. Oppressed people invariably respond by attempting the same oppressive tactics in reverse.

One of the functions of oppression, of the acceptance of oppression is an inability to deal with any other member of your oppressed group in an even one to one relationship. So it has got to be either you oppress me or I oppress you.

That's a constant factor that you've got to be aware of. You can't battle it or defend yourself against it; you can only neutralize it. Sometimes you have to say pure and simply, "What is it that you want that I have? There's something else happening here." Audre Lorde '77

At the same time, I discouraged the airing of grievances in the classroom.

Tensions were developing, especially the second week, between various people which led, I think, to some people withdrawing and others being angry. I can't honestly say that all of these tensions needed to be confronted either in the group or with only the involved parties. But I felt that the atmosphere of the Workshop, perhaps reflecting the problems most of us have in confronting others, was one which discouraged such confrontation. No one wanted to spoil the good supportive atmosphere; yet, by not risking its loss, I think we saw it as more fragile than it may have been, and thus came to trust it less than we might. Barbara Feldman

I was not censoring these messages but rather channeling them to face-to-face encounters between the individuals involved. If the class becomes an audience or a jury, the focus on our writing will collapse.

I was not available to meet in the dorms at night or to attend most informal discussion or readings. Sometimes people construed my absence after hours as a lack of support. Then they either grieved the loss of my friendship or else resented my absence. Yet if I spend more time with people, then they will be needlessly exposed to the intense daily Workshop pressures that I live with. While participants relax, I am constantly analyzing our experience, trying to determine the daily adjustments that will make our time together as meaningful as possible. Even in the tiny Pine Lake Workshop where I could not plead the pressure of numbers, I still spent most of my free time alone in my cabin. Despite its particular size or personality make-up, I need time away from the group.

For my rare social occasions, I sought out the "old Grads," women who had returned for their second Workshop. (Seven out of the original 22 women who stayed for the first Workshop in '75 returned in '76, traveling to Upstate New York from states as distant as Georgia and Michigan.) Seasoned with one Workshop experience, they became my source of advice and support. Unfortunately, these relationships generated an old girls/new girls split, construed by some as a divisive favoritism.

This jealously on the part of adults as well as my own panic when I felt misunderstood or unappreciated suggests to me that at times we might have been playing out conventional roles in an unconventional setting. As women we've been taught to regard each other as mothers and daughters, competing for the love and attention of the person in charge, traditionally a man. Or perhaps grieving for the forced divisions of mothers and daughters under patriarchy, the teacher's absence was seen as another abandonment. Possibly the teacher became the mother under intense pressure not to fail her children, experiencing anger or frustration as perilously inappropriate. The mother burdened by, possessive of the children who determine her social worth; the children dreaming of a smiling mother perpetually willing to play.

I get no writing done when I live in group—I'm either playing too much or upset that no one's asking me to play. (Yes, I use the word "play" deliberately to indicate the high amount of Child feelings that come out in me in new strange groups.)   Linda Brown

I felt very much like Adrienne Rich's description of a mother. Maybe it's the closest I've ever come to being in that situation. I admire almost all of them, even months after the event, but the very idea of doing anything like that again makes me shake all over.

One can't be a friend and a teacher and a sort of mother confessor all at once. There is really this tendency (which does not operate with male students and possibly doesn't operate in the ordinary academic setting) to demand so very much from a feminist woman who's older or who's in a position of authority, or teaching, etc. They really, most of them, expected you and me to be superwomen, which isn't a position either of us can fill. The work has got to be spread out, just like motherhood.   Joanna Russ '76

Finally, I am impressed by our willingness to forgive each other.

I'm writing to tell you how bad I feel that in our talk yesterday there was so much sparring and so little touching. It's a long leap from leader to person to friend, and I just wanted to jump a bit further in this letter.
                                                                             Elizabeth Kaye

Friendship

Between Ourselves

*I dig you, woman,
will keep you in mind & heart
as I write.*

Loraine Hutchins

It is impossible to separate the personal from the political from the professional. The Workshops focused on clarity and emphasized technical competence. Yet the sustained support of women we respected and grew to love as friends was a crucial element in the transformation of reticence into candor, of self-deprecation into eloquence.

For the first time I felt strongly what sisterhood is supposed to be in a large group of women: support, encouragement, and love for each other as women, as human beings who have the right to get the most they can from this world, and, in turn, to give the most they can to this world.
Lisa Bernstein

The Workshop is a continuing presence in my life. Just yesterday I felt the presence of Sherry strongly—as someone I could write to, as a woman who has perhaps made it through some of the things I struggle with now. I think of Loraine, Mary, De De and you. It's like I have some small stake in all our lives in that I want us all to succeed, not to compromise or to back down on whatever steps we must take for our full flowering artistically and personally.
Linda Brown

I feel reinforced in my prior feeling of the remarkable things that women can do together—I felt, from others, an almost immediate sense of support and enthusiasm, which made possible the intense sharing and trust that went on. I do not believe this could have happened in a mixed group, am positive that the level of understanding could not have been reached.
Dianne Chiddister

Despite the grim cinder block walls in the dorms, the participants asked to live together there. *

Getting to know the other women was for me perhaps the most valuable aspect of the whole Workshop, and I feel I got to know the women living in the dorm much better than the others. I don't suggest that dorm residency should have been required, but perhaps you should indicate to women the advantages of choosing to live in the dorms.
Kay Tipsord

When women register for an experience as short and intense as this, I would suggest that you strongly recommend—as part of your brochure material or personal conversation—that each woman live with the group and eat with the group. Don't feel it's not for you to say!   *Lisa Bernstein*

---

* Some women lived off-campus or in cabins at Pine Lake.

As we reveled in each other's company, we worried about departure. When Adrienne Rich visited again in '76, the first question that she was asked involved sustaining our women's community after the Workshops ended.

When we come here it's a communal celebration; we have a tremendous sense of togetherness. When I leave, I go back to isolation and loneliness. How can we sustain on a day to day basis as women and as writers—which is almost a double whammy—what we've learned here and shared here?
Pat McElligott

Traditionally, the great artist triumphs against all odds; alone in his garret, genius prevails. The wife who provides creature comforts and encouragement is reduced to a background figure of no note, who must subordinate her own genius to care for him. In this cultural scenario, we never had a chance. Further, we were trained to attribute our failure as writers to our own inadequacies rather than to a tradition that undermines our attempts to write, to think, even, about what we might want to write. Tillie Olsen was very much with us in spirit as we of the Workshops read her article on "Women Who Are Writers in Our Century: One Out of Twelve"* in the college library.

As for myself, who did not publish a book until I was 50, who raised children without household help or the help of the "technological sublime" (the atom bomb was in manufacture before the first automatic washing machine); who worked outside the house on everyday jobs as well (as nearly half of all women do now, though a woman with a paid job, except as a maid, is rarest of any in literature); who could not kill the essential angel (there was no one else to do her work); would not if I could, have killed the caring part of the (Virginia) Woolf angel—as distant from the world of literature most of my life as literature is distant (in content too) from my world.

The years when I should have been writing, my hands and being were at other (inescapable) tasks. Now, lightened as they are, when I must do those tasks into which most of my life went, like the old mother, grandmother in my Tell Me a Riddle *who could not make herself touch a baby, I pay a psychic cost: "the sweat beads, the long shudder begins." The habits of a lifetime when everything else had to come before writing are not easily broken, even when circumstances now often make it possible for the writing to be first; habits of years: response to others, distractibility, responsibility for daily matters, stay with you, mark you, become you. The cost of "discontinuity" (that pattern still urged on women by a society that prefers that they adjust, not itself) is such a weight of things unsaid, an accumula-*

---

* Tillie Olsen, "Women Who Are Writers in Our Century: One Out of Twelve," *College English* Vol. 34 (October, 1972): 13-14. The original of this article was a transcribed talk, spoken from notes on Dec. 28, 1971, at the MLA Forum on Women Writers in the Twentieth Century.

tion of material so great, that everything starts up something else in me; what should take weeks, takes months to write; what should take months, takes years.

Increasingly aware of the strikes against us, we became determined to work out new ways to succeed. Simply recognizing the facts of our oppression helped us to rebel with less guilt.

> Women going into rooms and closing doors behind them are breaking a taboo.
> Adrienne Rich '76

We questioned guest writers on practical issues, like childcare, that might affect our writing. Alice Walker, countering a lifetime's propaganda of Gerber babies and Hallmark cards, matter-of-factly explained why her novel *Meridian*, which she began when her daughter went to nursery school at age one, required five more years for completion.

> I had to get used to having a child. It was very hard to get used to having a second person around. Women who intend to have children should really make every effort to know what kind of plan will fit their needs. You don't have to get frustrated if you can think in terms of using other forms. You don't have to write a novel; you can write a short story. You can fit it in with a child. That's really crucial. Otherwise, you'll feel that you'll never be able to finish anything.
> Alice Walker '76

Recognizing our common problems as women writers helped us break through barriers traditionally dividing us, like sexual preference or race. Adrienne Rich spoke to us through a persona of a Russian woman in "Phantasia for Elvira Shatayev," where we assume that erotic love may be one aspect of women's friendship; a black woman, Alice Walker, spoke to us through Lynne, a white woman in *Meridian*. In class, Alice and I discussed the legitimacy of our creating characters not of our race and culture.

BT: In the past, I was made to feel insensitive or presumptuous if I identified with a black woman. I'm just beginning to see through this dodge. That community was denied to me because it was politically feasible to keep us isolated, to deny the commonality of our oppression.

AW: Lynne was a woman like me, she suffered under a man like I have or like Meridian has. In many ways, we're very much alike. In fact, from the time Lynne went on Welfare, there's very little difference between her and your average black woman on Welfare. Because the people who run this country could care less about her. No matter how white she is.

During other Workshops, we continued to question guest writers, interweaving the personal, political, and professional. With Grace Paley, some of us discussed our unwillingness to raise children and our subsequent ambivalence. In strongly supporting our choice not to become mothers, Grace rejected cultural stereotypes of the woman who is deliberately childless.

In *Enormous Changes at the Last Minute*, I have Dennis write a song for Alexandra that I took right out of *Isaiah*.

Sing, oh barren (woman).
For more are the children of your life
Than the children of the married wife.

You can relate to children whether you have them or not. And you can also not relate to them.   Grace Paley '76

We discussed our feelings of isolation and community:

GP: *Free yourself from the family and make your own community. If you're all alone, you can't do it. But you're not alone; you've had even this two-week workshop—and when you go further out, you'll find people just like yourself. You're living for a woman in the most marvelous time. There's nothing like the Women's Movement—and I've been in a lot of politics—for community and joy.*

BT: *Sometimes I do believe I'm the only person who feels like this. Until I remember I've met other women whom I write to. I'm willing to inconvenience myself a lot more than I used to. Because now I realize that if I don't drive two hours to meet someone for breakfast, I'm losing something of my life. If I don't make the effort now, it's going to be my fault.*

Extrication and Revelry

Being candid and a woman involves risk. At the very least, I may be met with disbelief or plain confusion. At the worst, I may be punished for my insight. Because of fear of retaliation or estrangement from people I love, perhaps I will limit my perceptions; I will not let myself know as much as I might under more supportive circumstances. Our community may very well determine the parameters of our wisdom.

Alice Walker inspired us by her loyalty to her own perceptions, and the implication that we must champion our own insight without regard to the prejudiced expectations of our readers.

I trust what I know has happened, not just to me but to people around me. I try very hard to remember my experience, even though years later, people will distort it . . . I'm not worried about what I'm trying to say. I'm worried about what I believe. If I figure out what I believe, I'll know what to say. That means I'm writing to be in communication with myself. The audience doesn't exist until way after I have gotten from the book what I wanted.   Alice Walker, '76

Yet, many of us cannot always willfully obliterate the presence of an audience we know will be hostile or unreceptive to our work. Consequently, we may not record what we actually want to say or we may not give ourselves permission to even think about what we might want to record.

I remember in a graduate writing workshop often being confused by positive feedback that overlooked my intentions. In one particular poem, I focused on the narrator's anger with a lover who grieved over the collapse of their relationship and over the loss of all the good times that he remembered. In reality, the narrator left him because of the misery of his repeated infidelities and deceit.

Beverly Tanenhaus

The Last Love Song

You have written a poem for me.
It says that you feel sad
That we are not together.
It says that you remember
All the wonderful times.

This poem is shown to friends
Like a perfect snapshot.
Exposure:
A colored depiction
Of how good things used to be.

Me
Ditched between the sheets
Trained for calm good-byes.

You
Jumping out of bed
To meet a girl for lunch.

Me
Squeezing my thumbprint on your heart
According to direction.

You
Bending down to kiss my hair.

Me
Examining my body
For evidence of breakage.

You
Shutting the door
On your way out.

These are the pictures, love,
I'll carry in my locket.

    This advanced writing workshop admired the poem but found it psychologically inaccurate. As men, they could not reconcile the submissive behavior of the first person narrator in the poem with the angry statement of the poem itself. One man summarized for me my inconsistency: "Lucy Locket wouldn't have written that poem." The only other woman in the class felt that the anger was overdrawn.
    Later, there was immediate validation by feminist critics of the psychological portrait of this poem. The narrator was identified as another self-conscious victim whose only consolation becomes the documentation of her pain. Here is the "eloquence of helplessness," ultimately self-destructive unless it leads to an acknowledgment and eventual rejection of the misery that some of us have accepted as daily experience. Another woman poet—Alta—responded to this poem with only one critical impera-

tive: "Bitch, sister, bitch!"

This example illustrates the support women are giving and getting in women's community, the support that characterized each of our Workshops. Women's friendship is as important as sound criticism. What helped me to stop writing and living poems of victimization was the support of other women who genuinely cared about my life, who were not threatened or unnerved by my intense emotion, and whose examples of personal strength suggested new female images in my work and my life beyond the eternal losers and sad ladies of establishment literature. And, in this reciprocity of power, my insight reflected back to them the possibilities of their own lives.

Women's poetry is beginning to be addressed to a community of other women, to individual other women. These poems simply assume a woman reader. They're not speaking over the heads of women to some man out there, who might be listening. This is very different from a female poetry which is still trying to explain women to men.   Adrienne Rich '76

The impact is so dramatic when we move into women's community precisely because we are extending the parameters of our wisdom and, consequently, changing the way we live our lives.

I read the evaluations today and thought: this is what friendship is—a loyalty among all of us, an alliance with truth; we promised we would stop lying. Because we made this commitment, together and joyously, our lives are bound in such a way that, even if we never see some of the women again, we'll have shared a vital moment in each other's lives. You're right; memories of the Workshops will never be merely nostalgic.   Pat McElligott

Community among women can serve, I'm learning, to organize those of us with common interests and support us as we take our own risks in our personal lives.   Clara Jones

We realize that we must extricate ourselves from the patriarchal definitions of women, from the dreams we were force-fed. This is a complex process for many of us that may involve our acknowledgment of how deeply we relied on men to make us feel good, to make our lives seem valuable. It requires bravery and candor to admit how oppressed we are and to find the courage to reject this oppression and work our way to something new or newly retrieved. On the other hand, we revel in the strengths we knew we always had that were trivialized, denied, or devalued by the culture; in the strengths we are developing now that we have given ourselves permission to be powerful, "unfeminine" women.

The Workshops helped me see myself in a way I never really had before—women knowing their power and daring to acknowledge and use it . . . I have this faith that something is gestating in me that will alter my life as a consequence—only I don't know what it is or when it will appear. So much goodness and strength absolutely has to be building something!   Elizabeth Kaye

Joyously, we are deepening friendships between us, now that we are free to reject their image of us as expendable creatures, merely keeping casual company, as we await the kiss of the prince.

The ramifications of this extrication and revelry may be drastic. They may involve a painful reconstruction where we must float along bad memories in order to accurately grasp the past so that we can truthfully record our experience.

I'm in the process of writing a new short story, more difficult than "Rites of Passage" because it involves three major and a few minor characters, has shifting scenes and covers about a year in the characters' lives. It's been a prodigious effort partly because the story's complicated and because I don't have the moral support of the Workshops. But mainly because as a writer I've made the startling discovery that I have to relearn my past.   Pat McElligott

I remember specifically when I was ten years old, the daughter of my mother's forelady (at the steel plant where she worked) was to take her nursing licensing exam one Saturday morning. I prayed the entire time of her test that she would do well. Obliteration of the self, yes indeed, when I could have been outside exploring the world, filling myself up and learning. There I was—closeted. I remember reading a book from the St. Stanislaus Parochial School Library about children who were martyrs and identifying with them, praying like they did on my knees on a hardwood floor, back straight, hands clasped.   Aldona Middlesworth

For many of us, re-examining our past involved re-examining our sexuality, and ultimately changing our definitions of love and power. Just before the first Workshop in '75, I typed several poems by participants on ditto sheets so that class discussions could begin immediately after arrival. The explicit depiction of sexual themes in these poems impressed me. Actually, my fingers had never typed such daringly erotic lines. I remember thinking that, as a typist, I was surely passing through some initiation rite.

As things turned out, we were profoundly touched by the shared documentation of our sexual experiences. In fact, our moral consciousness was transformed by what we had to say to each other. The lesbians among us deeply affected the straight women, as one by one they came out in their work. In '75, successfully socialized by a heterosexist culture, many of us reflected a naivete, damaging to ourselves and our sisters.

Women's love for women has been represented almost entirely through silence and lies. The institution of heterosexuality has forced the lesbian to dissemble, or be labelled a pervert, a criminal, a sick or dangerous woman, etc., etc. The lesbian, then, has often been forced to lie, like the prostitute or the married woman.

. . . Heterosexuality as an institution has also drowned in silence the erotic feelings between women. I myself lived half a lifetime in the lie of that denial. That silence makes us all, to some degree, into liars.
        Adrienne Rich, Women and Honor: Some Notes on Lying

After years of sexist media, it had not occurred to some of us that we could be madly brushing our teeth for anyone but the boy next door. As one participant stated, "My concept of my sexual self had always been my father's."

Our friendships with women whom we admired and respected, who had happily chosen to love other women, invalidated major tenets of our past—that a woman could only be turned on by a man's sexual domination, that lesbianism reflected tragic emotional pathology. In '75, our revelation centered on the fact that loving women might be a valid sexual choice, a distant or lost possibility. Recovering a part of our adolescence, we laughingly speculated on sexual technique, etc. By '76, the abstract erotic possibilities of a lost youth had become for some of us a much more immediate issue. "Does loving a woman mean I make love with a woman?" echoed through personal conversations and through individual poems. Several women came out after each Workshop, and one woman left her husband to move in with her female lover. She commented, "The Workshop didn't make this decision for me; it only moved it up two years."

Whether we actually became sexually involved with another woman or theoretically accepted lesbianism as a valid, pleasurable choice for women like ourselves, our rejection of heterosexist taboo radicalized us. We began to reclaim our bodies from the patriarchy and to acknowledge our beauty as independent of male decree and manipulation. No longer restricted to a traditional context where we functioned sexually for male pleasure or procreation, we began to write intimately, accurately about our innermost parts. Our genital imagery emerged as powerful metaphor in the world outside our bodies, as illustrated in the following passage in *From An Old House In America* that we heard Adrienne Rich read live in '75 and on tape in '76.

the rose and violet vulva of the earth
filling with darkness

yet deep within a single sparkle
of red, a human fire

and near and yet above the western planet
calmly biding her time

By experiencing other women as the essential resource, we redefined the sources of power in our lives. Never again would our destinies exclusively depend on men, for we had found each other. Consequently, we realized that the frenzied edge of heterosexist romantic passion was neither inevitable nor imperative. Although we might acknowledge men as a valuable part of our lives, we no longer gave them the power to define our lives. Backing away from the desperation of compulsive heterosexual coupling, from a debilitating "femininity," from actual madness, we were no longer Daddy's Little Girls in the Kingdom of the Sons but rather sisters, reclaiming, reaffirming our lives through our writing and through continued acts of friendship.

This song is a statement of eternity for this workshop, for this group of women together. Nobody can ever take that away from us.   Paula Gills

SINGING FOR MY SISTERS

WORDS & MUSIC BY PAULA GILLS

BRIGHT LATIN BEAT

VERSES
1. I've been looking all my life for a song to take me higher than I've ever been before. I've spent so many useless nights wasting time in crowded barrooms singing songs to some back door.
2. I've been feeling lately like there's something waiting for me that I've never seen before. It's my reflection in each woman's face I see that brings me to myself that makes my song mean more.
3. I've been looking all my life for a song to take me higher than I've ever been before. So come and sing this song with me, come share the love and celebrate the struggle we live for.

REFRAIN But WHEN I'M SINGING for my SISTERS there's a glow within my eyes that lights up all their hearts and warms the love we realize. When I'm singing for my sisters I feel all the power start to rise and watch the strength within our souls open up the skies

D.C. 1st & 2nd time

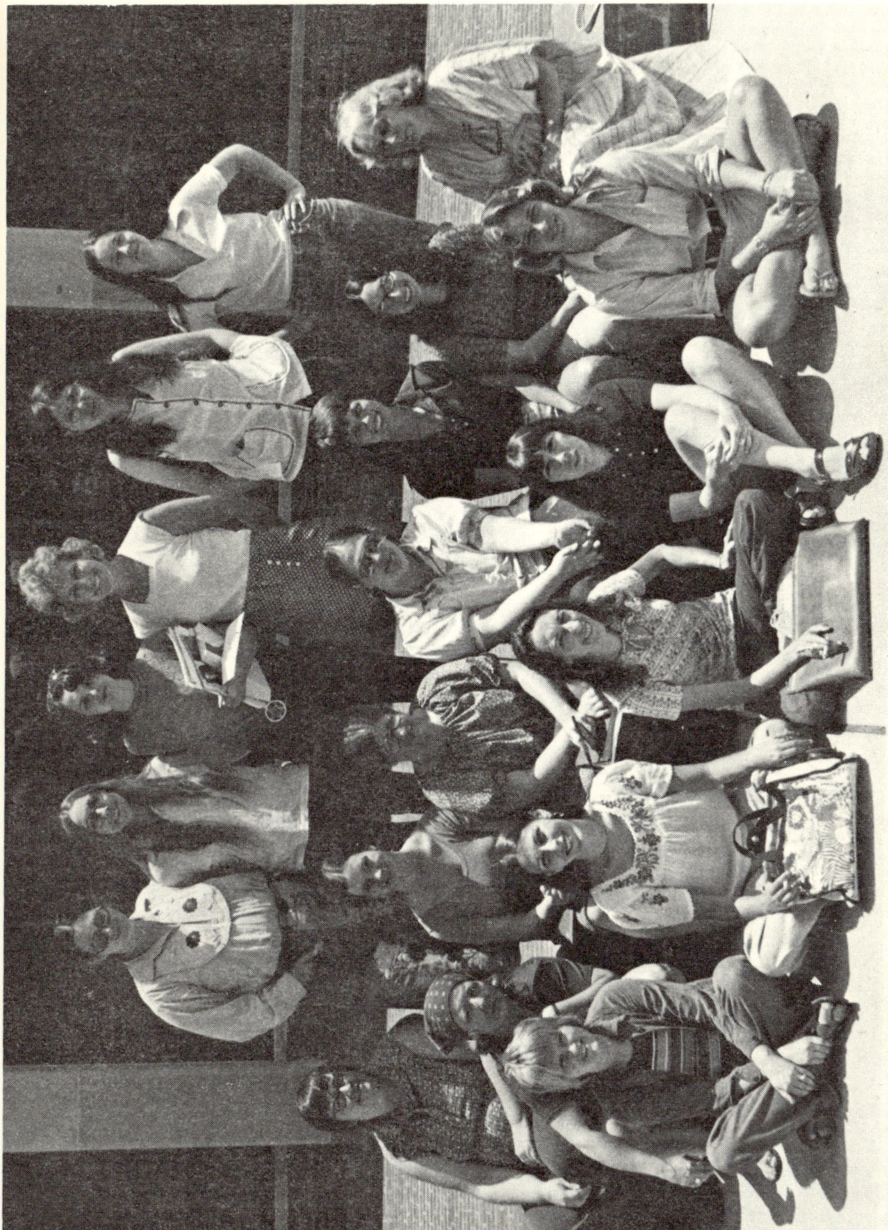

In a few weeks my son will be back, I'll have to face a classroom of young male faces. I have to care about them, and I do. Yet I resent the energy that caring takes from me. You see, I haven't really made my "re-entry" yet. Is there a way not to?   Sherry Redding

Re-Entry

During the Workshops, the alchemy of our insight had drastically changed us for the good; we looked forward to harvesting our memories after we returned home.

At the end of the Workshops, I was so nurtured, I felt I could do anything.
Melanie Perish

The Workshop was a free space, a sacred space for me to remember and come back to whenever I get scared about taking myself seriously as a writer. I hope to be part of such experiences again and again.
Loraine Hutchins

Yet our euphoria at finding new friends, renewing our commitment to our work, and realizing significant artistic growth, at times, changed to frustration in the outside world. The intense pleasure of each other's company at the Workshops emphasized the cost we paid in our daily lives for the lack of women's community.

I brought back to Detroit many feelings, one of which surprised me: anger. Anger because the kind of support, validation, and indepth criticism that the Workshops fostered is not readily available to women. What I am seeing now is how this lack, for myself and for other women I know here, has stunted us and continues to make change and growth very difficult.
Barbara Feldman

When we encountered people who did not even begin to grasp or who contested the value of the Workshops, we felt disappointed or betrayed. It irritated us when we were asked to justify our enthusiasm for a women's writing community to people baffled or offended by an experience that temporarily excluded men.

I found myself really lambasting a woman who thought that an all-women workshop "wasn't quite right." Yes, I would have had these responses before the Workshop, but I could tell from my language, from the immediacy of my responses that I have more commitment, better articulation, and much less tolerance for those kinds of people and conversations.
Melanie Perish

When I got back here a woman asked me why I wanted to go to a writing workshop at all and why did I have to go to one that was all women. I couldn't even think of how to answer her because all the reasons seemed so obvious to me. It's just a place to go to be with my sisters; that's the only answer I could give, and I know it wasn't adequate.   Kay Tipsord

Sometimes we regarded these questions as a costly distraction, as an attempt to reorient us to male definitions in which our own experiences were →

I started to feel the real power, the strength of my voice; then I was absent from the group for one day. When I returned to the Workshop I felt my sense of self begin to dissolve. I felt that no one was interested in me or my comments. I was coming from the outside, instead of looking outside with my own eyes.   Aldona Middlesworth

In fact, some of us refused to relinquish or tone down our new self-confidence. We determined to re-arrange our priorities to favor our identities as writers and feminists.

We saw our unwillingness to dilute our new ideas, our refusal to needlessly compromise in order to appear less threatening, as an act of courage. Others saw our bravery as abandonment. The all-comforting mother with a thousand arms became a woman using both hands to type. Our commitment to writing changed us from the constantly available helpmate with no important projects of her own. Or our serious consideration of women's issues disturbed men who feared that our anger toward them might become a terminal statement, stranding them on the wrong side of separatism. Or they resented our loyalty to our sisters as threatening their stronghold over our emotional lives.

Consequently, many of us, after living with women for two weeks, arrived home, out of practice with the delicate balances of subordinating ourselves to another's ego. The difficulties of coordinating our own expectations with the expectations of others from our domestic and professional past often confused us.

The whole thing has been an experience that I would not trade for a book in print (how 'bout that!). Yet despite this, both years I have come home and proceeded to have my personal life and my creative life go through a period of difficulty if not catastrophe, and I don't exactly understand why.
Kay Tipsord

If friends don't share my eagerness, my joy, it cuts the heart out of our relationship because writing is the single most important subject in my life right now. Almost every other topic (except sex) seems tepid in comparison. I have an overwhelming desire to be surrounded by people who can discourse brilliantly on craft, fiction, Adrienne Rich, etc. I haven't gone mad, but I do feel a painful need for relevant conversation, moral support, a springboard for ideas, and the conviction that I can live with my other friends even if they are artistically indifferent.   Pat McElligott

I remember attending a dinner party with a few friends just after the end of one Workshop. In buoyant spirits, I shared some of the Workshop highlights. Eventually, I realized that I had alienated every person in the room with my undisguised enthusiasm for what I belatedly recognized as subversive ideas. I found myself angrily defending radical feminism to a man who had been a friend and lover, and, at that moment, had painfully metamorphosized into an enemy. After the sustained support of my sisters, I had discarded an apparently crucial social skill—the diplomacy of reassurance—in favor of simply pursuing my own ideas. I realized then that often belittled or overlooked.

We weren't quite as nice or as patient as we used to be.

what had often struck us as flashes of brilliant insight at the Workshops may have been insights we were not able to admit to consciousness previously.
 These tense confrontations with strangers, the burdened intimacy with old friends and family, troubled us, sometimes resulting in periods of self-doubt. Yet, our faith that our insight was valuable, deserved, and ultimately moral remained intact.

> So much has been expropriated from women. When we begin to write out of what actually is happening to us as opposed to what's supposed to be happening to us, will that too be expropriated? Only with the growing awareness of and growing contact with a female community does one get the strength to know they can't take it away from us because it isn't just mine; it's all of ours. They can't take it away from all of us.
> Adrienne Rich '76

Specifically, we attempted to devise networks of communication between us to sustain our feelings of Workshop community long after classes had ended. Remembering that letters have been an unacknowledged genre of women, we vowed to overcome our inertia and regularly correspond.

> I am more alone here at home than I was before I left for the Workshops, but I don't feel it half as much. I have more of myself to rely on; I have the knowledge that there are interesting women I know and may be able to turn to. Knowing that they're there is a sense of possibility that I haven't had for awhile. And writing letters has been a way to keep the Workshops from becoming some lovely moment in time, to keep it from becoming a precious experience that I hold on to instead of use. By writing letters to women in the Workshops I acknowledge the power of the Workshops, the power of women in community, because their effect and importance become an ongoing condition in my life.
> Melanie Perish

Seven of us decided to exchange new work (or else a letter) on the first of each month. Then we agreed to mail out critiques by the first of the next month. Although this Writing Exchange is a lot of work, it's a crucial way to stay in touch as well as to get critical feedback. For little-known writers, thoughtful audience response reassures us that we are being taken seriously by women we respect and therefore must continue to take ourselves seriously.

> We wanted to keep the dialogue going and we have, in a most intimate way, through the exchange of our work. Last month packets arrived in my mailbox a day at a time. One by one I opened six envelopes and out slid these gems, this manna from heaven! I was overjoyed to hear from everyone, to share our work and our thoughts. It encourages us to write because we know we have an enthusiastic, caring audience in Georgia, Michigan, New York, Pennsylvania, and Washington D.C.—links in a chain that holds strong (for me) against isolation. Tillie Olsen once told us that the small victories we gain are so hard to sustain on a day-to-day basis. Here in Pittsburgh I feel your connection, your closeness, and it fills me with a sense of calm that sustains me.
> Pat McElligott

Admittedly, our Writing Exchange has lapsed on occasion; at this point, almost a year later, only five of us still steadily correspond. Yet, in an inhospitable culture, without the support of my sisters, I am at the mercy of my own self-doubt. Sometimes I contemplate devising a test for artistic genius, which will finally reveal me as a fraud. But then I receive carefully documented critiques of my work or else the personal responses to my discouraged letters. "You should write because your poems help me live my life." Isn't this the support we all need to continue?

After '75, I invited editors from women's presses as guest speakers for each Workshop in order to communicate publishing possibilities as well as document the evolution of the feminist media. If each of us is to truly experience writing as the "communal or tribal act" described by Adrienne Rich, then we must become aware of the alternatives to the Cosmopolitan Girl, to the mass-marketed beaming housewife. At first the lyrically exotic names of feminist pulications like *Chrysalis, Sinister Wisdom, Heresies, WomanSpirit* enchanted me simply as magical incantations; eventually, I realized the importance of subscribing to them. *The New York Times Book Review* is not going to give us what we need. But the investment in feminist press publications and magazines, the pilgrimages to feminist bookstores keep up the life of the community; our revelations continue through the mail.

In order for all of us not to be isolated, we are going to have to make a concerted effort to stay on the mailing lists of or in communication with the women's media because that is our lifeline. Maybe we all have to create our own archives.   Adrienne Rich, '76

Finally, armed with addresses and book lists, bonded by community, we re-entered our daily lives with our manuscripts meticulously typed and our notes in order. Clearly, the women of the Workshops had gained the self-confidence necessary to struggle seriously as writers. If, as the teacher, I emerged as an expert in taking other people's writing perhaps more seriously than my own, I too flourished in the community's powerful affirmation of me as an individual. As Martha Ficklen wrote, "I know myself a little better. I accept myself with a little less protest." I began to reject my identification with the waif abandoned at the train station, or the misfit stupidly defying the crowd. Instead, I saw myself as a powerful woman attempting changes that I knew were appreciated and reflected elsewhere by other women.

Once again, mingling the personal, professional, and political, Workshop participants report back the shifts in routine that alter a life.

I have decided to teach my summer school women's authors in English Literature from a feminist perspective, and I have started harrassing men who harrass me.   Paula Gills

In the afternoon, Mara and I walk up and down the road where there is a soft pink flower called hardhack in bloom, goldenrod, and a few old daisies covered with dust. We read, and I work in my garden or wander around outside while Mara picks green tomatoes and digs up unready onions. It is important that she have a sense of herself, even at two; that she be trusted. So I try to let her alone.   Valerie Kern

> Organizing a women's writing workshop with high school women is perhaps the first thing I've done where some sense of larger commitment has overcome my sense of personal protectiveness. I'm interested in the lives of my high school students and their work, their lives via their work, their writing as a part of their lives. I need to know if young women are growing up in a different way and if they are, how. Time and again last year I kept writing on their critical papers, "You are an articulate woman; you have a responsibility to document your age." I believe that—believe it of them because I believe it of myself and know that I never could have believed it of myself if I'd not had the forum of the Workshops both years to nurture that belief.
> Melanie Perish

In Adrienne Rich's *Phantasia for Elvira Shatayev* the Russian women are not snowbound skeletons, lost to us on a massive mountain.

> Every cell's core of heat   pulsed out of us
> into the thin air   of the universe
> the armature of rock beneath these snows
> this mountain   which has taken   the imprint of our minds
> through changes elemental and minute
> as those we underwent
> to bring each other here
> choosing ourselves   each other   and this life
> whose every breath   and grasp   and further foothold
> is somewhere   still enacted   and continuing

As women bonded by the recognition of our worth, the value and beauty of our words, we hear each other across country; across the turned backs between us, our loneliness is shared, our wisdom is lucid, as the tribal cries translate eloquence into joyous survival.

Elizabeth Kaye

After Hearing Kate Millet

Yeast working through the mass
requires warmth
Give yeast more heat,
it begins to expand,

creates transformation,
draws air into immobility,
rises to defy gravity—
naturally—
springs up like a child
into an adult body

Ready now to nourish
and make sweet
like cake, like bread,
like a loving woman

We are the leaven,
we are the salt,
and we are very savory.

Melanie Perish

Arriving for a Visit

You have moved away from the house
where my adolescent voice
richocheted off sewing room walls,
penciled itself in messages
on the formica table next to the stove:
        who called
        where you were
        when I wanted to get up.

Now, muffled shoes follow your voice and the gold rug,
step between coppery sofas, early American tables, the dust-free lamps;
Your smile surveys your well-chosen pieces,
nourishes the roses I had delivered from town,
rests on my pen and ink newly framed above the bookcase;
Standing at the dining room table,
we talk in new prints and old:
        How are you feeling?
        Does Papa like Pittsburgh?
        Do you have someone to talk to? Did you
        when I was a little girl?

You give me a seed pearl necklace,
sharp heels clicking contentment on kitchen tile,
your careful stories of my childhood;

You say I must be tired
after my long flight.

Hugging you, a kiss for each cheek,
I go up to the guest room,
close the door half-way;
I cannot hear you move with sink water rushing
though I know you've not taken off your shoes;
Eying your sewing scissors
I want to
cut the knot separating each pearl,
Lance your stories with a match-cooled needle,
push out the fluid
just under the skin—
But there is no time for repair,
no time to heal,
no reason to give you nothing.

To Look at My Hands and See

I've the hands of a single woman
broad palmed, fingers slender,
nails short, but filed,
and looking at them

I see
hands that never knew a pencil,
the hands of a woman
living in Dubrovnik
that sewed sails with a fishbone needle,
boned the catch with a knife,
mended socks at night by an oil lamp
as she sang young children to sleep;
never knowing that calloused fingers
would wave grown daughters good-bye,
clutch her cross and kerchief
as they sailed
with their husbands
for America.

I see
my grandmother
living on Fullerton Avenue,
her hands red and chapped
from washing other people's
shirts and dresses, sheets and towels,
hands that locked together each night
and in the incense-heavy church
praying for more work
and the Depression to end;
hands that animated stories
of gypsies in Slavic seaports,
that never learned to write
anything in English
but her name.

I see
my mother's hands
unpacking cartons of dishes, boxes of toys
each time my father transferred;
they worked quickly,
smoothing sheets, filling cupboards,
ordering my world, my sense of home;
and I never wondered
how often these hands
clenched in fists, in anger
she would not allow herself to own
as she heated bottles,
gripped the black handle of a steam iron,
carried her Bible to church;

I knew only the fingers
that touched my back as I studied,
held the books she read to me,
that carefully turned the pages
of everything I wrote.

I look at my hands,
the blue vein pulsing,
well-muscled fingers
holding the notebook,
part of the pen's movement,
able to
speak her silence,
write more than her name,
word her unstoried value;
I must grasp their unlettered lives
to begin to embrace my own,
grateful to them
that I'm able
to look at my hands and see.

Melanie Perish's After Statement

What impressed me about Alice Walker was the genuineness of her presence—not only that she was unaffected, but that it was clear from her manner and the things she said that she was a decent woman working from a definite moral framework, who had come to the Workshops to share her work and her thoughts with other women. She said a great many valuable things that continue to stay with me. One was that "in questions of morality, I have to ask myself 'What is good for the child?'; the child is the center of my morality." As a woman, as a girl-child, the roots of my own morality came down to me through women and I think that's some part of what my own poem is saying.

"To Look at my Hands and See" is a poem that recovers a personal herstory, a personal matrilineage that spoke to me. What's more, it reflects my concern with the women in my own heritage who certainly had the power, but often did not have the language or the belief in their own experience to do the sort of documentation I would so love to have now. And in the month of writing and rewriting that poem, I thought often of the discussion we had after Adrienne Rich's second reading; I knew that I could not let lives so close to my own be lost. I needed to acknowledge their importance to my own life, needed to recognize the differences, to emotionally and linguistically bond them to my own in the hopes that other women would feel that need as well.

Martha Ficklen
Aunt

My aunt set her table with one plate.
I would watch her pinch juice from a lemon wedge
   onto buttered, broiled fish,
Slip her fork under asparagus spears that all pointed the same way,
And I'd think to myself if I lived alone I would eat potato chips
   from the bag without bothering to sit down.

She bathed with monogrammed soap.
In her closet hung long nightgowns, clouds of peach and pearl,
That she wore to sleep alone.

In the bottom drawer of her bureau she kept for me
   a box of Sunbonnet Sue paper dolls, tracing paper,
   colored pencils and sewing scissors, with points,
   that fitted my hand.
We made wardrobes together.
She rocked and knitted, eyes closed to the light I needed,
   knowing her needles could work without surveillance.

Her hair was white at forty and I thought she was old.
At night she placed a metal clip with four porcelain teeth
   in a dish beside her bed.
She never talked with them out of her mouth.
I associated the appliance with her silence,
Like the springs of a music box removed.

Now at seventy-three she is younger.
She leads a lobby on rights for the retired,
Travels, dresses dolls for great-grand nieces,
Addresses college alumni at banquets.
We hear her coming in late evenings,
Setting out her tea and plate.

Beverly Tanenhaus

To the Daughter I Became
Who Gave Birth To The Mother I Needed

A mother who croons an epic lullabye,
I rock you in my arms, for all
The years I lived before I bore you.
Daughter, when you became part of this air
I had already learned to apologize
To dread what I feared I couldn't do.

I have lived those failures
Before you were born.
Before I met you
I cried at five years old,
Terrified by the complex twisting of my name
The day in school I had to use the alphabet.

At ten
I waited a week
For the drug store to develop
Pictures from the miniature camera
Bought for a dollar on the street.

I was ready
For the miracle
Of that tiny machine, ready
To admire the souvenirs
That came from my own fingers
And my careful eye.

I never told anyone
That only a blurred roll of negatives
Recorded my accomplishments,
Already accepting
Failure as my inheritance

Believing
Intimacy with things gone wrong
Would be my grief.

In the spring
I was not surprised
That the tulip bulbs I had planted
Toward the center of the earth
In our backyard hill
Did not survive the winter.
Colorful flowers
On packets of seeds
Belonged to other people
With better fortunes.

I never owned another camera
Or grew a garden.
If I could not succeed
Then at least I would not fight my pain.
I would be gracious.
This self-defeat was praised
As old wisdom in a young girl.

Love, you did not witness
The misery of those years.
Today, my African violet pleases you
With its green leaves like a litter of healthy pups.
You admire the photographs on my walls.

Do not accept a repetition of this story.
Leave my history behind.
Forget the years between us.

Come into my arms
And believe we were both born
Always acknowledging our gifts.

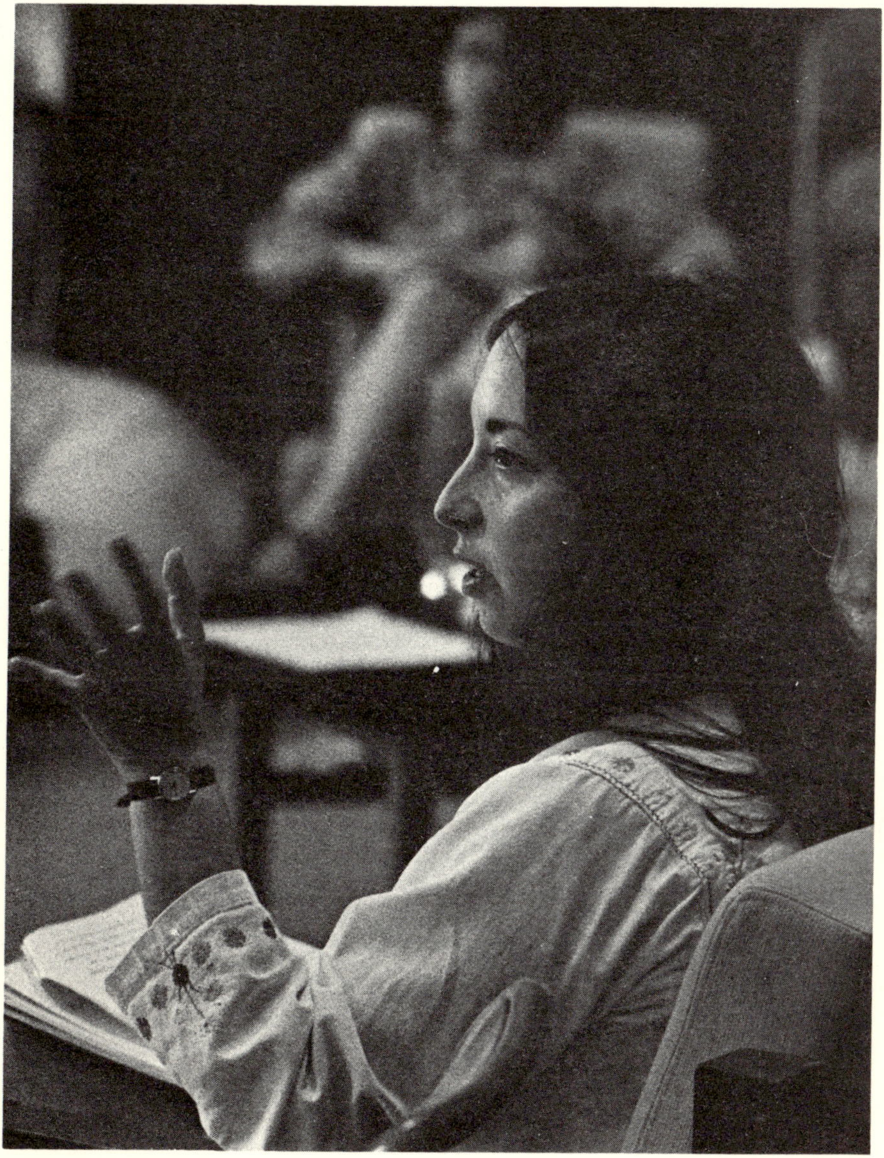

Beverly Tanenhaus was born in 1948 in Binghamton, New York. With degrees from Cornell, Johns Hopkins, and Brown University, she has taught creative writing to undergraduates, adults, and children. She is willing to organize and/or teach in women's writing workshops anywhere in the country. Her poetry has appeared in small magazines and anthologies including *Sinister Wisdom* and *Cameos: New Small Press Women Poets* (The Crossing Press, 1978). Her feminist literary criticism has been published in academic journals.

Women interested in attending future Women's Writing Workshops should write to Beverly Tanenhaus c/o Hartwick College, Oneonta, New York 13820.